BEYOND
THE CLUTTER

Discovering Personal Authenticity

DAVID WIENS

Beyond the Clutter

Discovering Personal Authenticity

Copyright © 2009 David Wiens

ISBN-10: 1-897373-70-8
ISBN-13: 978-1-897373-70-5

Unless otherwise indicated, all Scripture quotations are from The Holy Bible, New King James Version®, Copyright © 1982 by Thomas Nelson, Inc. Used by permission. All rights reserved. Scripture quotations marked (NIV) are taken from the HOLY BIBLE, NEW INTERNATIONAL VERSION®, NIV® 1973, 1978, 1984 by International Bible Society. Used by permission of Zondervan. All rights reserved.

Italics throughout have been added by the author.

Published by Word Alive Press
131 Cordite Road, Winnipeg, MB R3W 1S1
www.wordalivepress.ca

WORD ALIVE PRESS
Just Write!

To those searchers after truth who,
having been wounded in their quest,
find it difficult to trust again.

ACKNOWLEDGEMENTS

With deep appreciation to my wife, Elsie Anne, who continues to be my great encouragement, and best friend through the various seasons of life.

> *The sun sparkles bright off the dark-petalled trees,*
> *In a world that's refreshed by the rain.*
> *A rainbow shares luster, suspended by breeze –*
> *The storm has passed by once again*
> *And just when it seems that life's storms will not end,*
> *My soul is refreshed by your love.*
> *The dark sparkles bright because you cared, my friend,*
> *God's love hangs a rainbow above.*
> *The glory of God spreads its radiance all round –*
> *The storm has passed by once again*[1]

Special thanks to my mentor and friend, Steve Masterson, who provided an environment that allowed me to *'see my first gopher.'*

Thanks to many individuals who, by their thoughtful kindnesses, made a significant contribution to my life – and to the completion of this book.

Thanks to my heavenly father, who works all things out for good to those who love him.

---

[1] *Reflections on the Storm* an unpublished poem by David Wiens.

TABLE OF CONTENTS

An autobiographical sketch of the author's journey that took him from trying to find his identity through performance to discovering that he did not know who he was.

An exploration of the human soul, and how the events of life impact it, resulting in the development of a false identity based on performance.

An exploration of how traditional Christian doctrine, and less-than-diligent biblical interpretation may well be contributing to an identity crisis in Christendom.

An autobiographical sketch of how the author discovered his true identity through a divine gift.

An exploration of doctrinal concepts that are biblical, and foster a growing identity in Jesus. Those living in the paradigm "Grace and Truth' may well draw different conclusions from those in the 'Right vs. Wrong' paradigm.

PREFACE

"To be, or not to be, that is the question."[2]

For the past half century it has been my privilege to be an active participant and observer of the Christian church in its many forms and facets. Each facet appears to be a departure from the others in an effort to proclaim the gospel in a way that provides a new freedom in Christ, while eliminating other issues that are seen as dead weight. And, it appears to me, as each of those efforts has been institutionalized, it has tended to become the albatross around the neck of its wearer, becoming an object of worship, rather than the message of love that was originally intended. It is my conclusion that each, in its own way, ends up adopting a legalism that says, " We are right, others are wrong," that leads to a departure from the message of Jesus, when he said,

> *"You shall love the LORD your God with all your heart, with all your soul, and with all your mind. This is the first and great commandment. And the second is like it: You shall love your neighbor as yourself."*[3]

Jesus not only affirmed the centrality of love, but also that it would be the Holy Spirit that would empower

---

[2] William Shakespeare
[3] Matthew 22:37-39

his followers to love. St Paul's experience was that "the *love of Christ compels us*'[4], implying that it overtook him the way a disease might hit him.

Traditional Christianity, not having had that experience, has made love a choice – something one does because it is the right thing to do. Indeed, with the institutionalization of Christianity, the organization gravitates to a 'Right vs. Wrong' paradigm, regardless of truth, creating in its followers a false identity based on performance.

The true church, that community of followers of Jesus, lives in another paradigm – introduced by Jesus when he appeared full of grace and truth[5]. It is my belief, and growing experience, that when one moves into a 'Grace with Truth' paradigm[6] – the paradigm of the open heart – the heart receives the love of God, which then radiates to others. This paradigm cannot be institutionalized, since it arises out of a personal relationship between Jesus and his individual followers. These individuals may meet corporately, but they do not become slaves of organization and performance – their identity is a gift of creation. In the following pages, we will look at these two paradigms, and explore the process of transition from one to the other.

---

[4] 2Corinthians 5:14
[5] John 1:14
[6] Since this is a difficult concept for those in the' Right vs. Wrong' camp to grasp, see Appendix Four for an illustration of the difference.

INTRODUCTION

Enter by the narrow gate; for wide is the gate and broad is the way that leads to destruction, and there are many who go in by it. "Because narrow is the gate and difficult is the way which leads to life, and there are few who find it.[7]

As I examine the words that Jesus chose to use in this discourse with his disciples, a picture of a carnival emerges in my mind. I am standing at the gate amid the clutter. My purpose is to visit a display at the far end of the grounds.

At the entrance I am faced with a broad space occupied by booths with hawkers pushing their wares; with a midway where one pays to go round and round and yet end up at the same spot; with beautiful displays and exhibits – all clamoring for my attention. It is a place where many would try to mould or shape me, a place where it is easy to lose my identity as I blend in with countless others being swayed by their environment.

But for me, because I have come with purpose, the gate is very narrow, and all that occupies the fairground becomes obstruction or clutter standing in the way of my goal. Thus the gate becomes a place of resolute determination, a place where I must take a stand lest I

---

[7] Matthew 7:13-14

become sidetracked and miss my goal. The broad way must ever be that space of distraction between the place where I now stand, and the place where I reach my goal.

But even as I 'pick my way' between rides, around booths, past beautiful displays, I experience tension with those wanting my attention. If I do not give in, I may experience some distress, even persecution, because I am not living up their expectations.

Having been taught that Christians are to walk along a lonesome, narrow path, while the others are on a wide highway leading another direction, I had not been prepared to find the narrow path leading right through the clutter of the broad one. Nor did I realize that the Christian church might well have booths set up at the carnival - booths that would be particularly alluring because they have a semblance of spirituality.

But it did, and I was distracted. Consequently, much of my years of service in the church may well have been spent 'dancing with clutter'. But God, in his mercy, opened my heart and renewed my mind, and now I see the picture more clearly. The truth is that He is calling me to receive his love so that I may love and enjoy him and his creation - and extend grace to fellow travelers still distracted by the clutter. That, for me, has become the narrow path.

> *"I press toward the goal for the prize of*
> *the upward call of God in Christ Jesus."*[8]

---

[8] Philippians 3:14

CHAPTER ONE

Identity Lost

If there were no real love,
there would be no counterfeit.

It was a different time. No paved roads, not even gravel. The dirt roads turned to gumbo when it rained, clogging up any wheels that dared move on them. And when it was dry, the roads were rutted and rough, with hard clods that really hurt bare feet, even for young boys who ran barefoot all the time. Cars were becoming increasingly popular, but horse-drawn wagons still frequented the roadways. The odd horse-drawn carriage could still be seen but no one thought to run after the horses to pick up the 'road apples' they left behind. However, tires would run over the manure, flattening it, as the sun and wind dried it, till it turned into a warm, soft pillow – very comforting to bare feet. Such was life in rural southern Alberta in the fourth decade of the last century. A young barefoot lad, his clothes clean, but patched, stands on such a pillow and wishes that the whole road were paved with dried horse manure. Then, running barefoot would be such a pleasure. Heaven's streets might be paved with gold, but for a young barefoot lad on the prairie, dried horse manure seemed quite adequate. I was that lad.

I had another longing, not as pronounced as the first, but nonetheless present – deeper, more constant. As far back as I can remember I have had a longing to know truth, particularly the truth of Scripture. As a little boy I wanted to go to church. I remember, on one occasion, asking my dad to take me. For some reason, he hesitated. I suspect it had to do with my shoes, which were so shabby my toes stuck out. But I insisted that I would go barefoot, and he relented. I remember neither the walk to church, nor the truth being expounded, but I do remember standing beside my Dad as he sat in the pew. I could barely see over the back of the pew ahead of me. I remember nothing of the service, but I still see the little boy standing next to his dad in church, feeling so proud.

The community in which I lived included many German-speaking folk – mainly farmers who had arrived in the 1930's hoping to acquire cheap irrigation land offered by the CPR. They were people who shared a traditional conservative Christian faith, who grouped together and built churches to propagate their faith – and their language. My understanding was that German-speaking folk went to church regularly – English-speaking folk did not (not that we would have known - the nearest church offering services in English was some twenty miles away). Add to that, the belief among the German-speaking folks, that sin was geographically localized; in the dance hall, the pub, the pool hall – but not in the church, or the post office. The result was a polarization in the community. From a religious perspective, this created a mentality of 'us/them' for both language groups – a mentality the church I attended did very little, if anything, to dispel. As a result, friendships within the church group were encouraged – friendships outside the church group were not.

To propagate the language, the church folk offered German School on Saturdays. I was so thrilled that my Dad held the view that five days of public school, and one day of Sunday School were enough, so we did not have to attend. In recent times I have wondered if his reasoning had more to do with longing for a church community that transcended language barriers. But he never spoke about it, having the wisdom to stay away from controversial religious issues. His concentration was more on being a friend to anyone who needed one. But because he did not attend church regularly he was not considered to be an insider in the church community. Consequently, at my parents' farewell from the area, though it was a community event hosted by the church, the most profuse accolades were offered by non-churched folk. I was so proud of them.

Since the church I attended held to the doctrinal view that everyone is born a sinner, having inherited guilt from Adam, there was a lot of emphasis on "getting people saved". Saved from what? Hell, of course. There was a lot of emphasis on hell as well. So there were annual evangelistic meetings where a guest speaker would come and preach to the converted – few, if any, others attended. Sometimes in moments of greater clarity, they were referred to as "deeper life meetings", so the converted could benefit as well. I particularly remember one evangelistic series that ran every evening for a week. We had moved to a farmstead about half a kilometer from the church, but for some reason I was not required to attend, though we were within walking distance. It was during the heat of summer and the church windows were open. The speaker was eloquent, and though the church did not have a PA system, we could clearly hear him from our house. I asked my mom why he shouted so loud. "Did he think the people in the church were deaf, or something?" I found her reply rather surprising. She said that he was trying to communicate with people, who, like a certain alcoholic in the congregation, were very hard-hearted, and would not listen to reproof. So it became necessary to speak loudly – very loudly. That did not make any sense to me. If you want to communicate with this man, why not speak with him privately in a language he does understand, rather than shout at him in a public meeting? But I was only ten, and the depth of Christian religious practice was still foreign to me. I was, however, being introduced to clutter.

Nor did I escape becoming a target for evangelism. I, too, on several occasions was confronted with the question, "Have your sins been forgiven? Have you asked Jesus into your heart?" If I knew the questioner well, my response was, "No." That way, the pain of the conversation was reduced, because a short salvation prayer later, I was again on my way. If the person did not know me well my answer was, "Yes." Then, after a short prayer of encouragement, the question was dropped.

The questioners I took exception to, however, were the traveling evangelists, who would end their presentation with questions like, "Does anyone here want to live closer to God? If so, put up your hand." For me the obvious answer was, "Yes." Why would anyone take the time to hear an evangelist if they did not want to live closer to God? I thought everyone's hand would be up. But they were not – though mine was. Then came the hammer. "Now, would all those who put up their hand, come forward to receive salvation." It was not a question, but an assumption. As a twelve-year-old, I was deeply offended. I had enjoyed the presentation. I had enough trust in the presenter to admit that I wanted to walk more closely with God. Now I felt betrayed. The memory is very vivid. I was so tempted to tell the evangelist he was a liar trying to manipulate his audience. Instead, I got up and left the assembly, hoping no one would have seen my upraised hand, since "all eyes were closed and every head was bowed." It would not be until four decades later that I would hear an invitation that I thought was honest, loving and sincere – the evangelist was the late Terry Winters. How I miss that man!

In addition to the Hell and Salvation themes, there was a lot of talk in the church that I attended about God, service, spiritual growth, service, obedience - and service. I do not recall ever hearing a message about love – though surely someone must have touched on the topic. There was some emphasis on co-dependence, though – it was improperly called love. It went something like this, "If you don't love someone, start praying for that person and start doing nice thing for him/her. Before long he/she will be doing nice things in return, and you will love each other." It is not difficult to understand why this type of teaching did little to produce a congregation of loving people – and yet, some were.

Nor was Jesus mentioned much in adult circles. He was someone to believe in for salvation, but it seemed that God and the individual took over after that. I can recall as an adult how awkward it felt as I began to talk of Jesus as my friend.

Having 'become a Christian', the next step in sanctification (becoming holy) was to be baptized – immersion being the proper way. On the farm of one of the church deacons was a stock watering hole. This was fitted with a handrail, to assist those going into and coming out of the water. Baptisms were somber times – a step of obedience and an expression of Christian piety. I made application when I was in my mid-teens. It required giving testimony to one's faith before the church congregation. Then the church members debated the candidate's eligibility. Generally the prognosis was positive, and baptism could proceed. This usually became a special service down by the watering hole.

I really wanted it to be a meaningful experience. But I was not a swimmer, and the stale water was cold. And my head had to go under. The cold water seemed to knock the breath right out of me. I did survive, however, in spite of the huffing and puffing as I tried to regain my breath. In the dressing room, the kindly pastor asked me if I was experiencing the joy of the Lord yet. Though I was not, I did not want to admit it, so I mumbled something. "It will come," he said. "In time it will come." It was a prophetic statement – a prophecy that would find fulfillment some thirty-five years later.

Church membership followed automatically after baptism. As an official member of a church I now had a sense of belonging. Because my work in the church had value, it gave me a sense of value. I poured myself into service in the church – singing in the choir, teaching Bible studies, teaching extension Sunday School, getting involved in youth work. Later, I would serve on church boards, direct choirs, dramas, musicals, and concerts. In fact, I married the church, and she became a hard taskmaster.

I have just used the term 'church', a word that seems obvious, but in reality is more complex than one might realize. Let us divert for a few paragraphs while we examine the concept of 'church'. What do I mean when I say I married the church?

The word 'church' in the English language can mean a variety of things. The most obvious is a building, usually with a name on it indicating that it is a church. If that is what you meant when you said you went to church, it would probably make better sense if you had said you had gone to a church building. In days past, the concept was clearer. People met in a meetinghouse. And that is precisely what a church building is – a meeting place. It is made of the same building materials that are used to build hotels, service stations, fire halls, and houses. It may, however, be dedicated to a sacred purpose.

Those who see the building as a place where God dwells are living in the religious philosophy of the Old Testament times. They tend to call it the 'House of God'. In ancient Israel, God wanted to live with his people so he had them construct a dwelling place for himself that became a symbol of his presence with them. However, St. Paul writing in the New Testament era, suggests,

7

> *"God, who made the world and everything in*
> *it, since He is Lord of heaven and earth, does*
> *not dwell in temples made with hands..."*
> (Acts 17:24)

In this age, God wants a more intimate, personal relationship with his people. St. Paul continues,

> *"... do you know that your body is the temple*
> *of the Holy Spirit who is in you, whom you*
> *have from God..."* (I Corinthians 6:19)

It would appear, therefore, that God is only present in the building when his followers are assembled, and bring him with them.[9]

A second meaning of the word "church' identifies with the name that appears on or near the church building, indicating what organization happens to operate there. If the name says THE FIRST AMEN CHURCH OF TUMBLEWEED, you can now infer that the organization that runs the church, and possibly owns the building, is associated with the Amen Denomination. This building happens to house the organization of the first congregation of this particular denomination in Tumbleweed. The denomination is the parent organization that contains within it many of the smaller organizations known as 'churches'.

The church is usually registered with the government, and its bylaws will specify such tidbits as

---

[9] Matthew 18:20 "For where two or three are gathered together in My name, I am there in the midst of them."

how many people are on the Board of Directors, and how these directors are placed on the board. The bylaws will also state conditions surrounding the borrowing of money, and the dissolution of the establishment. There is nothing sacred about the organization.

How would the Christian religious organization look compared to the cereal shelf of a super market? The shelves could be compared to the church buildings, since they house the product. The cereal is divided into two major categories, hot and cold. Since the cold cereal has many more varieties, and can be consumed in many different ways, let us compare Protestantism with the cold cereal aisle – other Christian religious organizations with the hot cereal aisle. The manufacturers of the cereal would correspond to the denominations. As each manufacturer produces numerous products, most basically similar except for taste, and appearance, so each denomination contains many flavors of the same basic product based on locality and leadership. Nor is it surprising to find two almost identical products, made by two different manufacturers, similar in most respects except name. So too, one might find two very similar church organizations that display different denominational names. Hence, one can choose a flavor and a texture that seems appealing at the time.

What is noteworthy, however, is who runs the organization. Since its success is measured in terms of performance ratings, goals, and objectives, it tends to attract performers who want to make a difference in their world. Their lives are 'purpose driven' – they want to make a difference for God, and organization is the way it will happen. They reason that if they can have influence in operating the institution, they can ultimately change their world. Furthermore, since there is a right and a wrong way to operate an organization, the leadership will tend toward legislating what is right, and punishing whatever is seen as wrong. Any program or performance that enhances the institution is to be applauded. The members like to believe that God is on their side.

The adherents call themselves Christian, and display many of the appropriate qualities, but often these qualities are self-generated because the institution teaches that they are desirable. Unity is emphasized because looking good is important. Conflict is not allowed, lest the façade fall away, and baser motivations be exposed.

I expect that those who have been 'disappointed by the church' would say that it was actually the institution that has not met their expectations. They were looking for something it was not able to produce. And indeed, all the organization can produce is a system within which one may operate – a system that will eventually dominate and control.

A third use of the word 'church' identifies it with that community of people who enjoy relationship with Jesus. They know no geographical limitations. They are neither limited to one particular denomination, nor do they all attend the same church. Generally, however, part of this community will meet within a given church building, with another part in another church building, and thus support the local church organizations. Another part may meet within a home and worship there. Jesus said that this community would be known for its love. Its members display love and compassion, are attracted to relationship, and feel a kinship with other members whenever and wherever they may meet around the world. These folk have experienced the love of Jesus and, having received it, can freely pass it on. They believe Christianity is a relationship, between its founder and his followers. Generally speaking, they have no organization, are not attracted to positions of influence, but will effectively serve as the occasion arises. In this case, one does not go to church, but one identifies with church. This is the biblical meaning of church.

When these people join the organized church and move into administration, they will often find themselves at odds with the organization, and under pressure to resign. If, however, in the rare event that these people are the administration, and are not perverted by it, I suspect that even the building in which they meet will reflect a warmth and peace that will elicit reverence.

So, when I mentioned that I had married the church, what did I mean? While I thought I was identifying with the community of Jesus-followers, I was actually drawn into the establishment. In my efforts to know God better, I had been seduced. Unwittingly, I had become a performer in Christian religion with total allegiance to the church, rather than a celebrant of Christian faith. I had been seduced by clutter.

Was I becoming holy? No one seemed to know. For me, one of the distinguishing characteristics of the Christian religion is its inability to define holiness. We are encouraged to strive for it – whatever that means – but we are not expected to ever get "there" till we die. And how would we know we were "there", if we did not know where "there" is.

I recently met a man who teaches seminars on holiness. In my curiosity I asked him to define holiness for me. "Well," he said, "it's being set apart, being different, being sanctified." I then requested a definition of sanctification. "Well," he said, "it's doing holy things." But how do I know what holy things are if I don't know what holy is? "Look," he replied, "it's all in my teaching manual, and I don't have my book with me. It's at home." Needless to say, I was not any wiser.

The need to die to self is another major tenet of conservative Christian religion. Was I dying to self? I must have been. After all, I subscribed to the acrostic:

1. **Jesus**
2. **Others**
3. **You**

--in that order. And for years I carried a poem in my wallet that went like this:

Others, Lord, yes others, may this my motto be,
May I live for others that I may live for thee.

Again, the concept is problematic. Generally in these circles, self is defined as the sinful nature, because I am a born sinner. So how do I give that up, if that is precisely what defines me? Do my good works for others not suggest that I have given up self, or could they be indicative of an absence of self, so I define myself by my good works? The eulogy at many of the funerals I attended certainly suggested that it was the good works that defined one as a Christian. I learned that when one has no concept of 'self' to define the quality of service, it is indeed the frequency of service that becomes the definer of self. Hence, the more involvement, the more value – but personhood is totally lost.

One fact seemed rather obvious to me. There is a right way – and a wrong way. Generally the message was, "Avoid the wrong way, at all cost. Don't get involved with it." Rarely, when wisdom and experience were present, the message became, "Choose the right way, and stick with it." But, because no explanation was given, I was left wondering what might be the defining characteristics of the "right way". Would I recognize it if I saw it?

When one's religion is based on the foundation suggested above, there is a great need to depend on the mind to produce a logic that tries to make sense of everything. Hence, there is a danger of using Scripture to prove a preconceived idea (no matter how much the context suffers), and then to believe that idea to be right (not necessarily truth, but right). I suggest it is this need that empowers systematic theology. This often leads to a legalism that takes us right back to an earlier memory – if you can't communicate with them, shout louder. But the shouting did not answer my many questions. So I would move on to another location, hoping to find answers there. But when you are not sure of the questions, and questions are not encouraged, you lose faith in those around you, and there are few answers. Such is the dilemma of truth seekers caught in the clutter of Christian religion.

What I was not aware of at that time was that our perceptions determine our beliefs, and our beliefs determine reality for us. Dr. Luke graphically illustrates this concept in his gospel account of two of Jesus' disciples walking along the road to Emmaus after Jesus' resurrection[10]. Their belief that Jesus was dead was so strong that they were not open to receive any other message. Consequently, when Jesus joined them on the road, they did not recognize him, though they enjoyed the discussion with him. It was when he broke bread at their house that reality hit. Jesus was indeed bodily with them, and very much alive. Luke concludes,

> *Then their eyes were opened and they knew*
> *Him; and He vanished from their sight.*
> (Luke 24:31)

It is most difficult, if not impossible, for us to visualize something that has not previously been injected into our belief system. For example, some years ago, I had opportunity to travel across southern Saskatchewan with a young woman who had grown up in England. Though she had never seen a Richardson ground squirrel, (we called them gophers) or even a picture of one, she hoped to see some on this trip. That is not normally a difficult feat on the prairies, and yet try as she might, she could not see any. I pointed out many to her as we traveled, to no avail. She just did not know what to look for, but because she trusted me, she continued her search. After many

---

[10] The story is recorded in the Gospel of Luke, chapter 24 verses 13-35

miles, she finally saw her first gopher. Thereafter, she saw them everywhere.

My experience in my search for truth was similar. I had seen the mounds on the prairie. I had seen the little trails between the mounds. But I had not seen 'gophers' – nor did I know just what to expect. And when I consulted with those who I thought should know, because they were in leadership, I was met with contempt. It would seem that they had never 'seen a gopher' either, and were threatened by the thought that someone should propose something that was beyond the scope of their belief system. What complicated the situation was the fact that, in their minds, to contemplate something out of the realm of the accepted was to contemplate heresy.

On one occasion I heard the president of a Bible College announce that all truth contained in the Bible had already been discovered, and any new views should be considered heresy. I suspect he was referring to truth as accepted by western conservative Christians, to the exclusion of all others. It would appear that the delusion, indeed, runs deep. St. Paul encountered a similar attitude among the religious leaders of his day for he wrote,

> But even to this day, when Moses is read, a
> veil lies on their heart. (2 Corinthians 3:15)

When I was a younger man, the eight-millimeter movie camera and projector reigned supreme in the home movie field for those who could afford it. The pictures were developed on photographic film. One day, someone told me that he had seen a movie presentation (video was still an unknown word) being reproduced from a recording on magnetic tape. Since I felt rather confident in my knowledge of things electronic, and I did not believe a movie image could be reproduced from magnetic tape, I informed my friend that he had obviously not understood what was going on. He stuck to his story. I did not believe him, and could not fathom how he could be so gullible. In retrospect, I can see how those who are most convinced of the rightness of their beliefs are the least likely to learn anything new.

Jonah, of old, certainly spoke truth when he said,

"Those who cling to worthless idols,
forfeit the grace that could be theirs."[11](NIV)

And cling to worthless idols we do. Since our belief system is formed in our early years, there is danger that it may be built more on hearsay than on truth. Even when we attempt to research truth, our worldview conditions the interpretation of that truth to fit our preconceived reality. Since there is relative safety in the known, it is very risky to subject our beliefs to critical investigation. That is why having a trusted mentor is so important, and that I did not have.

The significant fact is, that by the time I was in mid-life, I found myself enmeshed in this very philosophy that was providing so few real answers. I had simply accepted it. And my 'Christian' service increased to a frenetic pace – I accepted a faculty position at a major Bible College. Much as I wanted to be a loving person, my worldview was one

---

[11] Jonah 2:8 New International Version

of contempt. The simple fact is that I had become a religious bigot. Because I could not see anything wrong with my philosophy, I must be right - always right. If you agreed that everyone should accept my conclusions, we could get along. If you disagreed with me, however, a power struggle would ensue in which I would attempt to prove you wrong. If I could not convince you, I would do my best to eliminate you - after all, you are the problem. It is an extremely contemptuous and irresponsible position. I honed my perfectionism, and I became the embodiment of a philosophy, which, though it was taught as the route to holiness, became anything but. All this I had done to protect my integrity. The man, Job, whom we will consider later, illustrates this philosophy well.

So here I was, nearly a half-century after the young lad had taken comfort on a horse manure pillow, now standing on a spiritual horse-manure pillow, shouting to all who would listen, "The whole road should be covered with horse manure. That way everyone could walk comfortably." Such is the clever deception of the Evil One – I was lost in the clutter.

The tragedy is that people caught-up in this life style really believe that they are serving God. They appear oblivious to the negative impact they have on those around them. Yet, this was the very lifestyle I had adopted in the absence of something better. At this point an experience brought me face to face with the fact that I did not know who I was.

The local school district was looking for a principal for one of its schools. I was qualified and unemployed – so I decided to apply. The first question of the interview caught me off guard, "So tell me – who is David Wiens." I had never before been confronted that boldly with the concept of my identity. I did not know what to say. I related some of my experiences as a teacher, knowing full well that I was not answering the question, only recounting my performance. Suddenly I was faced with the reality that I did not know who I was.

I pondered that fact a great deal, and wrestled with how I might answer it should I again be confronted with that question. I decided that saying, "I am a metaphysical absolutist and an epistemological relativist," might answer the question. But even then I realized that I was only defining myself on the basis of my beliefs, not on the basis of who I was.[12]

I have since discovered in the Scriptures that even God does not ask us to define who we are. He asks some very pointed questions: Where are you?[13] Why are you angry?[14] Where have you come from and where are you going?[15] Each is designed to stimulate thought about our philosophy of life. But when it comes to personal identity, he tells us who we are – and he should know, having created us.

You will have noticed that my 'growing up' experiences occur mainly within the context of the Christian religion. I use the term religion sadly but deliberately, because Christianity was never designed to be a religion. It was designed to be a relationship between

---

[12] A metaphysical absolutist believes in absolute truth, while an epistemological relativist believes interpretations of truth may vary.
[13] Asked of Adam, Genesis 3:9
[14] Asked of Cain, Genesis 4:6
[15] Asked of Hagar, Genesis 16:8

the founder and his followers. However, I would suggest that whenever a group codifies its behavioral expectations on the basis of right and wrong, and then tries to achieve the 'right' through personal effort, it subscribes to religion. There may be security in rules, and there may be a sense of belonging, but there is very little life, beyond that found in propagating the system – or violating it.

As a truth seeker, feeling disenfranchised, I was at a crossroad. Without a miracle, my future was predictable:

Sitting on the porch of life,
Rocking in the chair of complacency,
Watching the world go by
On the giant screen of regret and despair,
A little boy no more
But an old man
For whom the hands of time have moved too quickly

Sitting by the fork in the road
A tear slowly seeps down the side of his eye
And slips down the creases of his face
As he remembers all his hopes and dreams
He had planted so long ago
Being stripped away like leaves in a hail storm
And shattering like glass as they crash to the ground,
With the howling wind laughing and taunting
in his face.

Slowly memories come rolling out of the past
Like tumble weeds in time's breeze
Of love, that was like the beautiful
And delicate art work of the morning frost,

19

Beyond the Clutter

Now melted away by the heat of betrayal and mistrust.
The people at church,
Whom he sought out to quench his thirst for knowledge,
Only pushed him off the road
Into the dusty ditch without notice -
And then prayed for his soul.

Slowly over the years his mind's eye has grown dim
Partly easing the sharp pain
From the realization of opportunities missed.
He hasn't moved far from that fork in the road
Where he stood as a boy.
Once or twice he's gone a little way down the road
First one way and then the other
Only to turn back and return
Worrying that it might be the wrong way.

Now he just sits there in his rocking chair
Going back and forth as the dust slowly rises from his feet.
Time seems to pass him by now,
No longer even batting an eye at him,
For he's just a lonely old man
Rocking slowly beside the fork in the road,
As the sun slowly sets on his life.[16]

---

[16] *The Rocking Chair in the Setting Sun* by Bardo Wiens. An unpublished poem used with permission

CHAPTER TWO
Exploring False Identity

*You cannot give what
you have not received.*

Why, then, such a glum forecast? I was a respected faculty member at a well-respected Bible College, doing what well-respected Christians strive to do. For the answer, I needed to look deep into my soul.

Traditionally, the human soul is seen as having only three parts – mind, will, and emotion. Or stated another way: I think, I choose, and I feel. I would suggest that we would be wise to look a little deeper, and include two more characteristics, perhaps not as obvious, but likely as important. Hence, let us include the capacity of being able to relate, and the capacity to comprehend. In this case the soul has five capacities, represented by five interlocking circles as illustrated in Figure 2-1 following.

Hypothetical Model of the Human Soul

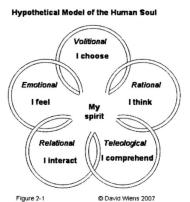

Figure 2-1   © David Wiens 2007

Thus I can visualize myself as a soul, housed in a body, energized by spirit:

- I am volitional – I choose, and I want to be affirmed.
- I am emotional – I feel, and I want to be loved and accepted.
- I am rational – I think, and I want to understand and be understood.
- I am relational – I interact, and want to belong, to be secure in relationship.
- I am teleological – I comprehend the end from the beginning, the cause from the effect, and I want to be significant.

Current psychological thought would suggest that the need to be secure (relationally), and the need to be significant (teleologically), is our deepest human need.

Figure 2-2   © David Wiens 2007

When my emotional need for love and acceptance is realized, I will feel a deep sense of relational security because I belong. When my rational need to understand

and be understood is realized, I will feel a deep sense of significance because I comprehend the big picture and how I fit into it. When this two-fold process happens with the assurance that I am made in the image and likeness of my Creator, and I enjoy relationship with him through Jesus, my spirit will be at peace knowing my identity is secure.[17] I am who he designed me to be.

When our spirit it at peace as depicted in Figure 2-2, it will be reflected by our lifestyle.

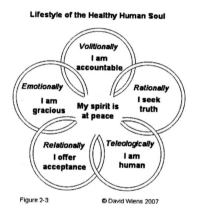

Lifestyle of the Healthy Human Soul

Figure 2-3   © David Wiens 2007

Decision-making in this situation will also be a two-pronged process. Because of the inner security I feel in relationship with myself, and my Creator, I will have a deep intuitive sense of what the reasonable response would be. Based on my sense of significance, I will trust my intelligence to evaluate the situation, and will find myself cognitively agreeing with my intuitive response. Hence, decisions will arise out of who I am and my

---

[17] The Spirit Himself bears witness with our spirit that we are children of God (Romans 8:16)

interpretation of the truth, not on what I think people expect of me. My choices will tend to be firm, while being in the best interests of all concerned. In short, I will act out of love. See figure 2-4 following.

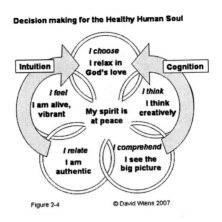

Decision making for the Healthy Human Soul

Figure 2-4   © David Wiens 2007

Unfortunately, we do not all find ourselves in this situation. We may find decision-making difficult. We may second-guess ourselves. We may spend a great deal of time trying to gain consensus from our peers. Our decision may change with every changing group we meet. We may fear being honest because it might reflect poorly on our being accepted.

In that case, the process in our souls will be very different. We will invest (often very subconsciously) in relationship to get what we want. We will manipulate and cajole in order to have our way. And though that may sound selfish, I would suggest it is a dominant characteristic of most relationships. How, then, does this come about? To find the answer, we must take a deep look within our own souls.

All of us have *longings*, though for many of us they may be suppressed to the point that we have no knowledge of them. These longings, I would suggest, arise out of our need to comprehend, and our need to relate. In short, our deepest longing likely arises out of our need to be significant, and our need to be secure in relationship. If we are affirmed, accepted and understood, these longings can be met. If not, we remain wounded. See figure 2-5.

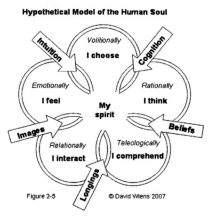

Hypothetical Model of the Human Soul

Figure 2-5   © David Wiens 2007

Now apply this thought to a child who is trying to make sense of a very confusing world. Visualize, for example, a little girl who really wants to be in relationship with her daddy. But Dad has to work outside the home and cannot spend all the time with his daughter that she desires. As he leaves the house, the little girl follows him, only to be abandoned when he drives away in his car, leaving her crying on the sidewalk. If this type of scenario repeats, the little girl, who longs for love and relationship, will begin to form *intuitive emotional images* or perceptions of abandonment. As the child tries to make cognitive sense of the images, her God-given ability to 'take dominion' activates, and she concludes that someone is at fault. She dare not blame the adult lest her whole world unravel. So she blames herself, and forms *beliefs* like: *'I don't matter'*, *'There is something wrong with me'*, *'It is all my fault.'*

The beliefs become a guiding principle in her life as she vows 'to be good enough' so that she will not be abandoned again. Since she cannot keep the vow, her negative beliefs are reinforced. She has entered the arena of shame, and will likely fall into a pattern of doing what she does best, whatever that may be, so she can never be accused of being inadequate.

Or consider the little boy whose drunken father beats him mercilessly, giving rise to a belief in the little boy that he is inadequate because he cannot stop the beatings. The shame associated with these beliefs is so severe that he may repress them, and may talk of the wonderful childhood he has experienced. Such beliefs are our best-kept secret, often being secret even from ourselves. Actually, I suspect that it is the deceiver who plants these lies in little children in order to control them. The child is now controlled by shame.

The effect in later life will be that the individual will shut down emotionally, while the unmet longing becomes a hunger that drives him/her into all manner of addictions. If I shut down emotionally, I will still feel anxiety, and I severely compromise my ability to find security in relationship. Furthermore, my ability to comprehend the world is severely compromised. I give up my power to those around me, hoping that by pleasing them, they will find me acceptable, and not abandon me, as I perceive my parent did. But I am never secure. I will be given to extremes. Either I trust no one, or I trust everyone.

Following are some characteristics typical of individuals caught in this perverse lifestyle.

- I am concerned about my reputation – I want people to see me as a nice person.
- I try hard to make people happy, and would never deliberately offend anyone.
- I am very uncomfortable with conflict, and will steer away from it if possible.
- I see 'idiots' all around me.
- I want integrity in my life, above all else (actually, I worship integrity).
- I do not handle compliments very well – they just don't seem right.
- I have great difficulty in receiving – I would rather invest than receive.
- My private life must be kept private.
- I am uncomfortable around people who are too emotional.
- I often have negative thoughts about myself - *I am stupid, I am inadequate, I don't matter, I am so dumb, I am unlovable, I am an idiot* – and, when I speak, I project these characteristics onto others without realizing it.
- I react defensively to a perceived challenge – I will counter-attack, or play the victim.
- I am very involved in serving my church, my family, my community, or some civic organization – in fact, in my saner moments I

might admit that I am too busy, but I don't know how to stop, because people need me to do the job right.

- I am uncomfortable around those who do not share my opinions.
- I concentrate more on piety than on devotion in my relationship with God.[18]
- My relationships, though they appear genuine, are really for my gratification.
- I am always right, and can offer advice on dealing with your problems.

Hypothetical Profile of the Wounded Soul

Figure 2-6   © David Wiens 2007

In Christian religion, this lifestyle will reveal itself through a number of roles the adherents play:

- A college professor or a pastor, who has no connection with the spiritual power to affect change in lives, will assume the role of teaching what is right and what is wrong.

---

[18] Devotion has to do with a deep, steady affection, loyalty and faithfulness, while piety has to do with religiously motivated performance.

- Keeping the doctrine pure requires a housekeeper, who assumes the responsibility of eliminating those in danger of thinking for themselves.
- The fan club pays the bills and says nice things about the leadership, at least in their presence. If a sermon creates shame in them - which it often does - they feel God is speaking to them.
- Then there are those caught up in the back draft. They do not agree with what is happening but, fearing that what is being taught might be truth, they hang around the periphery hoping something good will turn up.
- The disillusioned drop out quietly. They may have been actively involved at one time, but, not having been able to achieve their desired objectives, they fade into oblivion.
- The offended leave, not being able to tolerate the hypocrisy - often to form their own legalistic group that holds the previous group in contempt.

Lifestyle of the Wounded Soul

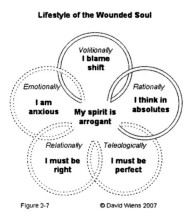

Figure 2-7 © David Wiens 2007

People in this lifestyle live in a 'Right vs. Wrong' paradigm. Being self-defensive, they will choose to be in positions of authority to protect their fragile ego. Rationally, they will blame shift. Teleologically, they will be involved in perfectionism. Relationally, they will initiate power struggles. And Emotionally, they will be condescending and arrogant to hide the pain of their anxiety. Though they may speak of love, what they practice is codependence. The tragedy is that in their own self-righteousness they do not see the truth about themselves. But their decision-making will reflect their condition.

Decision Making for the Wounded Soul

Figure 2-8   © David Wiens 2007

This, then, was the lifestyle I had adopted. I had joined the walking dead.

CHAPTER THREE

Fostering False Identity

If you cannot be true to yourself,
you will be false to everyone[19]

So how is it that a youngster growing up under the influence of Christianity ends up in mid-life with no concept of personal identity? Is Christianity not the most liberating philosophy known in the world? I believe that it is. But when it becomes perverted and is practiced as a religion, it becomes a dominating and depressing force in one's life. There are rules to keep, and expectations to live up to. I suggest that Christian religion, by its very doctrinal outlook, robs one of personal identity. Notice all of the negative identity statements in the following progression:

- I am born a sinner (oops!).
- I am given some reprieve till I reach the age of accountability.
- I am selfish from birth.
- I sin because I am a sinner.
- If the deceiver suddenly disappeared, I would keep on sinning anyway.
- I am swayed by peer pressure.

---

[19] Corollary to Polonius' advice to his son Laertes, in 'Hamlet' by Shakespeare. 'to thine own self be true, and it must follow as the night the day, thou canst not be false to any man.'

- Somebody leads me to Jesus.
- I confess my sins and accept Jesus as Lord and Savior.
- I die to self – a self I never knew.
- I do not know who I am.
- I am expected to be holy, so I fake it.
- I do not know how to love, so I pretend by being nice, rather than honest.
- I serve others for the reward, and become a sanctified co-dependent.
- Though I want to serve God, I really serve myself.
- I worship integrity and logic.
- Unwittingly, I move toward becoming legalistic.
- I support what is Right and abhor what is Wrong (in my judgment).
- I avoid conflict because it challenges my fragile ego.
- When challenged, I will blame and attack the challenger, rather than deal with the issue at hand – or beat myself.
- My self worth comes from my performance.
- I become a perfectionist – though I don't see it and would never admit to it.
- In my arrogance, I push people away. I remain an isolated island.

- I believe God really needs me to protect him and His operation.
- I stand on my self-made security cushion and try to rule my universe.

Foundational to the above paradigm is the statement that we are born sinners – a foundation, I suggest, that is at best dubious. For several years now, I have been looking for solid biblical evidence that this is a valid belief. This generally results in being given a list of biblical references - and contempt for even questioning this doctrine. But no one will talk about it. It appears to be a well-kept secret that only the initiated are privileged to know. Jesus suggested, *"If therefore the light that is in you is darkness, how great is that darkness!"* (Matthew 6:23) - and I am beginning to suspect that this doctrine reflects one of those dark situations. One church cancelled my Bible teaching privileges for questioning this doctrine, but no one in the leadership would even discuss the matter with me. The truth of an old adage appears to be reaffirmed, 'there is no heresy quite as dangerous as an ancient heresy'.

If indeed, it is heresy, it is most certainly a clever one. As it minimizes the potential of the evil one, it minimizes the whole spiritual battle we are involved in. Indeed, spiritual battle is reduced to in internal battle, which is fought between the individual self, and the sinful nature. And since the teaching is that the self must die, there is not much of a battle – the sinful nature wins hands down.

Let me suggest a reason why such confusion is common within the teachings of Christianity. Let us pretend for a moment. If you were the deceiver, would you rather have people believe what the Scriptures say about who it is that deceives everyone,

> *So the great dragon was cast out, that serpent of old, called the Devil and Satan, who deceives the whole world*; (Revelation 12:9)

or, would you rather have them believe that they are the evil ones suffering from their own sinful nature? The latter is precisely what the doctrine of original sin teaches. Once you can get people to believe that they are the cause of all the evil in the world, you are free to go raise havoc wherever, without being suspect or blamed. Neat trick, I'd say. In discussion of the above with a pastor friend of mine, I had suggested the possibility that we may have bought into a very clever deception. His response was, "Don't call it deception - a misunderstanding, perhaps, but not deception. Otherwise you are implying the devil might be involved."

As long as we have this attitude, I have no doubt that the deceiver will be involved. Consequently, one would expect to find other interesting interpretations being propagated as well, which we will get to later. After all, if you build a house on a poor foundation, you are sure to find cracks in the plaster sooner or later. But first, let us re-discover some history.

The debate about whether or not we are sinners at birth may well be older than Christianity itself. During the days of the prophet Ezekiel (circa 580 BC) a philosophy had become prevalent that suggested that children inherited guilt from their parents. Here is God's assessment of the situation,

> *"The soul who sins shall die. The son shall not bear the guilt of the father, nor the father bear the guilt of the son. The righteousness of the righteous shall be upon himself, and the wickedness of the wicked shall be upon himself."* (Ezekiel 18:20)

Actually God had already given his assessment years earlier through Moses,

> *"Fathers shall not be put to death for their children, nor shall the children be put to death for their fathers; a person shall be put to death for his own sin."* (Deuteronomy 24:16)

During the late second and early third centuries AD, Christian scholars began to formulate doctrine to create unity in the early Christian church. A man named Tertullian, who lived in Carthage, suggested that all souls were present in the seed of Adam, and since Adam sinned, all his offspring would be sinful. (I guess he had not read Ezekiel or Moses) It was as if Adam acquired a sin gene, and passed the condition along genetically to all his offspring. (Incidentally, there are people who believe this today, and suggest that when one becomes a Christian their genetic make-up changes.)

It so happened that Tertullian's views found favor in the early church in Rome, and hence, over time became part of the belief system of the Roman Catholic Church. During the protestant reformation, though some other dubious doctrinal issues were addressed, this one did not appear to get to the table, and so it became a part of Lutheran belief as well. Hence, it has become a major tenet of the Western Christian church, and has come to be widely accepted as fact in Christian religion.

It is my sense that we, in the west, have bought into a version of Tertullian's theory, and accept it as truth simply because it "always was". I suspect that if Jesus were involved in the debate, he would suggest that any effort to support this doctrine biblically would require "straining at a gnat, and swallowing a camel."[20] Regardless of our leanings, it is time to return to a serious exploration of biblical truth.

Those who believe this philosophy, base their convictions on a number of Scriptures[21], in both the Old and the New Testament, but most rely on the words of the Psalmist, David. After his affair with Bath Sheba, his neighbor's wife, and the murder of her husband, David's conscience was beginning to bother him more than a little. This, in part, is what he wrote:

> *Have mercy upon me, O God,*
> *According to Your loving-kindness;*
> *According to the multitude of Your tender mercies,*
> *blot out my transgressions.*

---

[20] For another view on this topic refer to: <u>Are Men Born Sinners?</u> by A.T.Overstreet http://gospeltruth.net/otherss.htm#sin

[21] Psalm 58:3, 51:5, Isaiah 48:8, Jeremiah 17:9

Wash me thoroughly from my iniquity,
And cleanse me from my sin.
For I acknowledge my transgressions,
And my sin is always before me.
Against You, You only, have I sinned,
And done this evil in Your sight —
That You may be found just when You speak,
And blameless when You judge.
Behold, I was brought forth in iniquity,
And in sin my mother conceived me...
(Psalm 51:1-5)

As you read on through the whole psalm, you will notice that it deals with the grief and loathing one feels when dealing with guilt. For the author to insert the last couplet above, and use it to prove just when he became a sinner is to suggest that the poet has a momentary lapse into the philosophical that totally violates the context of his poetry. It may, however, have something to do with generational sin.

Those who do use this as proof also tend to ignore other poetic statements the psalmist makes. Consider for example:

Yet you brought me safely from my mother's womb
and led me to trust you when I was a nursing infant.
I was thrust upon you at my birth.
You have been my God from the moment I was born.
(Psalm 22:9-10)

For You formed my inward parts;
You covered me in my mother's womb.

37

I will praise You, for I am fearfully and
wonderfully made; Marvelous are Your works
And that my soul knows very well.
(Psalm 139:13-14)

The above also illustrates another paradox in Biblical interpretation. We would like to believe the Psalmist when he states that it was God who formed us in the womb. But God is holy. Could a holy God form a sinful creation in the womb of a sinner? Would he? If not, under this doctrine every pregnancy is indeed a theological 'oops', while God looks the other way as another sinner slips into the world.

Another factor in the confusion arises from the fact that the most inexperienced theologians are charged with teaching the most impressionable in Sunday school. Because of the trust relationship with the teacher, most simply accept as truth that they are taught, and never bother to check for themselves even when they get older. Unfortunately, the teacher has often not checked, either.

Take, for example the story of Moses appearing before Pharaoh in Egypt.[22] God had shown Moses at the burning bush in the wilderness, that if his rod were thrown down it would become a snake (nachash in Hebrew), and when he grabbed its tail it turned back into a staff. However, when Moses tells Aaron to throw his staff down before Pharaoh, it does not become a snake, but a monstrous carnivorous beast (tanniym in Hebrew), likely akin to Tyrannosaurus rex. Imagine the scene in ancient Egypt – right in the palace, the tanniym of Pharaoh's

---

[22] Exodus 4:1-5, 7:8-13

soothsayers are being eaten up by the tanniym of Aaron. When the meal is done, the tanniym morphs back into a staff again. That should hold a kid's attention for a while. But I have never seen it depicted that way in Sunday School materials. Indeed, I suspect the traditional version contains both a translation problem, and an interpretation problem - but it is that version that sticks in one's mind.

Actually, I once met a man who knew the Hebrew language so well he would never read an English Bible. Rather he would read his Hebrew Bible and translate as he read – very fluently, I might add. One day he was elaborating on the concept of 'tanniym'. Because I love word studies, I had noticed the mistranslation in the Moses story. I brought it to his attention. "Impossible," he said, but he did not have his Hebrew Bible with him. I suggested he go home and check his Bible. He did. The next time we met he brought up the subject again, and agreed that there was a translation problem. "But," he said, "How could you possibly have known that, if you don't read Hebrew?" It was a rhetorical question and required no answer. But my question was, "How could you possibly read Hebrew and not have seen it?" That, I would suggest, is how the power of childhood memory keeps us from recognizing truth, even when it glares at us from the printed page.

But even Jesus' disciples experienced this phenomenon. Notice the following story:

> *Then He (Jesus) took the twelve aside and said to them, "Behold, we are going up to Jerusalem, and all things that are written by*

the prophets concerning the Son of Man will be accomplished. [32]"For He will be delivered to the Gentiles and will be mocked and insulted and spit upon. [33]"They will scourge Him and kill Him. And the third day He will rise again." But they understood none of these things; this saying was hidden from them, and they did not know the things, which were spoken.[23]

It would appear that they were so sure of what Jesus would do, they were unable to accept truth even when it was quoted to them from the Scriptures.

Currently, a common scriptural misinterpretation is our tradition of having the magi at the manger in the Christmas story. If you look carefully at the Biblical texts you will notice that it would have been impossible, without violating the text, for the magi to have seen Jesus before he was forty days old, and by that time the family had departed for Nazareth[24]. So if you want to see the magi worshipping Jesus, look in Nazareth.

Harmless stories, you might say. Perhaps, but I would suggest that unless we are willing to submit even our most cherished beliefs to the scrutiny of Scripture, we are in serious danger of departing from the truth. In fact, I notice, in a modern speech Bible translation my granddaughter just received, the text actually says the star led the magi to Bethlehem.

---

[23] Luke 18:31-34
[24] Matthew 2:1-16, Luke 2:1-7,21-39

It is of interest, as well, to note an interesting paradox when it comes to a belief in a Millennium (one thousand years of peace on earth still to come because the devil will be bound). The concept is based on the following Scripture,

> *Then I saw an angel coming down from heaven, having the key to the bottomless pit and a great chain in his hand. He laid hold of the dragon, that serpent of old, who is the Devil and Satan, and bound him for a thousand years; and he cast him into the bottomless pit, and shut him up, and set a seal on him, so that he should deceive the nations no more till the thousand years were finished. But after these things he must be released for a little while.*[25]

I must confess, I have difficulty in reconciling this Scripture with the belief that we are born sinners. Binding the devil will not affect evil on earth if evil is inherent within each of us, because we are born sinners. Millennium only makes sense if we believe that it is the devil that deceives the world[26] and that his absence will make a difference.

There is an interesting debate going on among those who believe we were born sinners. The theory goes that, though we are sinners, God does not hold us accountable for sin until we reach a particular age; some

---

[25] Revelation 20:1-3
[26] Revelation 12:9 ... *that serpent of old, called the Devil and Satan, who deceives the whole world...*

say three, some say five, some say seven, maybe more if some mental deficiency is present. They offer no criteria by which to determine this. Some say, "Have you ever seen anything more selfish than a baby?" Others say, "You can just tell." Yet others maintain, "That's the way it's always been." My question would be, "If God does not hold them accountable for sin at this age, why insist on calling them sinners? It's kind of like God saying, "You are guilty of death, you sinner, but you have such a cute button nose, and such tweaky little ears, and you are sooo cuddly, I'll just overlook it." That really doesn't do much for God's justice, does it?

And herein lies a most unique feature of this belief system. While it suggests that infants are exempt from judgment till they reach the age of accountability, I sometimes wonder if the age of accountability ever really comes. When I am fully immersed in the Christian religion, I will not accept responsibility for anything except my own piety. I am never wrong. Because I do not know who I am (having presumably died to self) I have become a most defensive non-person. I have become adept at blame-shifting the responsibility for any problems on others. Though I pride myself in my mature piety, I am still not accountable. The attitude is well summed up by the older brother, in a story told by Jesus. The younger brother has just returned home, to an unexpected celebration with his father, and the father invites the older brother as well. This is how Jesus framed the elder brother's response to his father,

"Lo, these many years I have been serving you; I never transgressed your commandment at any time; and yet you never gave me a young goat, that I might make merry with my friends. But as soon as this son of yours came, who has devoured your livelihood with harlots, you killed the fatted calf for him."
(Luke 15:29-30)

Such is the potential for celebration among those who are always right. Nor does the elder son accept responsibility for his inability to celebrate. He sees it as his father's problem for not giving him a goat, though he had already received two thirds of his father's wealth. What he failed to realize is that the gift was already his, but he was unable to receive it – typical of those caught in the 'Right vs. Wrong' paradigm.

It had also been my experience that Christian religion lacks a mechanism to deal with controversy. Invariably, the leadership demonstrates a very real fear of conflict. The solution proposed usually calls for repentance on the part of the one perceived to be guilty. In observing this, I have wondered why pastors and leaders had departed from Biblical principle, which surely they had been taught at Bible College. However, on further investigation and observation in the Bible College culture, I have come to the conclusion that the problem is not unique to churches. It is endemic.

Weakness calls for noise and zeal and ardor;
For show of force, defensive, resolute –

For every thousand who at leaves are flailing,
You may find one who's digging at the root.[27]

Might I suggest that fear of conflict arises out of a failure to believe that God can adequately meet my needs. In my insecurity, I try to maintain an uneasy status quo, rather than face the risk of being annihilated by new ideas that I am not prepared to consider, since they do not mesh with my belief system. Hence, I do my best to control the situation, and leave God to do his thing elsewhere. This is idolatry, pure and simple.

Also, in my quest for identity, my insecurity pushes me to please people so that they will see me as a nice guy/gal and there will be no conflict. So I give up my power to them, and allow them to define me. St. Paul speaks rather eloquently to this issue as well,

> *For do I now persuade men, or God? or do I*
> *seek to please men? for if I yet pleased men, I*
> *should not be the servant of Christ.*
> (Galatians 1:10)

Unfortunately, contrary to St. Paul's teaching, pleasing others is generally not seen as idolatry. But when we depend on people for our identity rather than on our Creator, there is no other word to describe it. It is idolatry.

Another area of confusion arises when the speaker has a good sermon, but he needs to find a text on which to hang it. Often there is none. I once heard a sermon on faith-promise giving. Afterwards I said to the speaker,

---

[27] Unpublished poem, Author unknown.

"Good sermon - wrong text." His response was that he was following a denominational outline, and this was the only text available. In that case, I would suggest the sermon just adds to the clutter.

An oft-used sermon text is recorded in Genesis 3:21 which says, *"for Adam and his wife the LORD God made tunics of skin, and clothed them"*. The gist of the sermon will speak of God's amazing grace in providing atonement for sin, in this case by killing a sheep, and clothing the couple with sheepskin – prefiguring the death of the Christ. That is indeed a good message. But I suggest it does not fit this text. The context is that Adam and his wife were living in a sterile environment, adequately warm and humid – an environment that had been prepared just for them, as they had been created.

I once asked a dermatologist, "Could a person survive in a sterile environment without the epidermis – the outer layer of skin?"

Her reply, "Of course not, our hospitals are far too polluted for that."

"No," I countered, "I said a *sterile* environment that was climate controlled and bacteria free."

"Oh," she said, "If you could create such an environment, a person should be able to live in it indefinitely without an epidermis."

I would suggest that Adam and Eve were created for precisely such an environment in the garden. However, when they arrived outside the Garden they were met with drought, heat, viruses, and weeds. God knew they were about to go into that hostile environment, where they would need a space suit to protect them – to regulate body temperature, to fight off disease, to maintain body moisture. And so God clothed them with human skin – in all likelihood he formed the epidermis. (It would appear that the dermis was already present at creation, leaving them looking somewhat ruddy. It is of interest to notice the derivation of the word 'Adam' means to be red or ruddy.) An alternate translation could read, "God made coverings of nakedness," and clothed them. So indeed, in spite of their sin, God's grace was offering them life, by covering them with their own life-sustaining skin.

Allow me a little rabbit trail. There is an interpretation tool called, 'The Principle of First Mention', which says that if you are wondering about the meaning of a word in Scripture, find the spot where it is first mentioned in the narrative, because its use there may inform you of its meaning in the rest of the Bible. This is the first mention of the word 'skin'. If you read that word to mean 'sheepskin', you may take an interesting journey through the Scriptures and substitute 'sheepskin' wherever the word 'skin' is used. It is most interesting when you find people having leprous symptoms in their sheepskin. Or Job having boils in his sheepskin. Or Ezekiel seeing the dry bones raised, covered in flesh, and clothed with sheepskin. It sounds like a bit of 'wolf in sheepskin', to me.

Though I have been referring to conservative Christianity, I would suggest that all of institutionalized Christianity suffers the same fate to a greater or lesser degree. The specific situations will vary. The discussions will be different. But each group has its own favorite view that it will seek to justify by referring to its own chosen Scripture.

The problem is that because our hearts are hard, we gravitate too easily from being an organism, to becoming sidetracked by the clutter of organization. Consequently, the intellectual mind tends to lack logic as it operates out of sync with the heart.

To further illustrate, consider an acquaintance of mine, then a leader in his church who prided himself in his logic, who had become angry with me, but had not told me. When he was confronted about it, some six months later, he said he had not approached me as yet, because he had been praying all that time for God to show him just how to approach me, and indeed he did not wish to be interrupted in that quest till he had an answer. I suppose he is still waiting.

My concern is this: when our hearts are hard, our intuitive sense is stifled, preventing us from hearing the prompting of the Spirit of God in our lives, leaving us devoid of wisdom, and depending solely on our intellectual capacity, which in this situation is not that rational. Phrased another way - wisdom is not attainable unless our intellectual and emotional intelligences work together in harmony.[28] When they don't, we move into a 'Right vs. Wrong' philosophy that is neither logical nor loving. This is the trap that is as old as creation itself.

Back in the Garden of Eden, when man and woman were created, they lived in relationship with God. In spite of being warned against being distracted by clutter, they

---

[28] For more on this concept, see Emotional Intelligence by Daniel Goleman, (Bantam Books, New York, 1995)

chose to eat the forbidden fruit – fruit that would give them intimate knowledge of good and evil if they depended on it for their sustenance. With the knowledge of good and evil, they no longer needed relationship with their Creator – they could determine their own destiny. This deception lies at the heart of the paradigm of 'Good vs. Evil', or 'Right vs. Wrong' as I refer to it. It is this very paradigm that motivates participants in Christian religion to work at earning their own righteousness – the paradigm in which I had unwittingly become trapped. I really wanted to love, but I did not know how.

I remember, on one occasion, attending a seminar where the speaker gave several lectures on the topic of Love. Between sessions I had coffee with him and expressed my anticipation of the next lecture. He wondered why. "Well," I said, "in the previous lectures you have told us about love. I expect that in the next lecture you will answer the question, 'How does one go about actually loving? How is it activated?'"

"No," he replied, "This is all there is. But from a practical perspective, a kick in the pants will do it for me every time." That was an answer that satisfied neither me, nor his wife who happened to be present.

I had learned, in talking with people who had been kicked in the pants, that this treatment produced anything but love. My experience was that it produced a bottled-up smoldering resentment. I left the seminar disappointed – more clutter.

Being a truth seeker in an environment of self-righteous piety is not easy. I had followed the tenets of Christian religion, as I understood them. I had served the

Church whenever I had opportunity. I trusted the leadership to provide Biblical answers. But still I felt that something was missing.

I had believed that God would affect positive change in my life, but I did not see it happening. And no one had the answers I was looking for. I had been kicked in the pants enough to know that more kicking was not the answer. What I needed was a miracle, not to smooth the road – smooth roads exist only in the imagination of the uninitiated. I needed a miracle that would provide me with a heart of tenderness and courage that could see through the clutter, and face life's realities honestly. But I did not know that such a possibility existed.

CHAPTER FOUR

Identity Restored

When you turn to face the light,
the shadows fall behind you.

"Then I will sprinkle clean water on you,
and you shall be clean; I will cleanse you
from all your filthiness and from all your
idols. I will give you a new heart and put
a new spirit within you; I will take the
heart of stone out of your flesh and give
you a heart of flesh. I will put My Spirit
within you and cause you to walk in My
statutes, and you will keep My judgments
and do them." (Ezekiel 36:25-27)

What I did not know at the time was that what I wanted was only available if I gave up what I had – the security provided by the familiar – though in my deception, I did not even know what I had. In retrospect I can see that I was firmly grounded in the relative comfort of the pillow on which I stood. The picture had not changed. Inside, I was still a little boy standing on a cushion of dried horse manure, wanting God to change the world so it would be comfortable for my bare feet. He, on the other hand, wanted to grow me so that I could handle life with all of its rough spots. And somehow, we were not communicating. Since God did not show much interest in my proposal, I could not trust him with my future. Again, since I was not interested in finding out what 'growing' meant, he was not about to show me. It was a dilemma that I was not even aware of.

The gospel writer, Mark, records a similar circumstance when he relates the story of a rich young man who came to Jesus asking the question, "What must I do to inherit eternal life?" [29]

And to Jesus' response, "You know the commandments," he replied, "I have kept those all my life."

Jesus replied, "You lack one thing. Go sell what you have, give to the poor, and come follow me." Not that he needed a perfect performance, but parting with that which was most dear to him, would free him from the idolatry of materialism, and indicate he had a heart ready to trust God for his future.

Looking back, I can see that I had to be willing to release my grip on my chosen foundation before God could do anything in me. I have come to appreciate the fact that God did not fulfill my childhood wish. Had he paved the whole road with something that would provide only comfort for me, and no pain, the deception I lived under would never have allowed me to even begin moving toward the truth.

And yet, when I contemplated leaving my comfort zone, to face the pain of "hard clay clods under my bare

[29] Mark 10:17-23

feet" it was, indeed, a major risk. In my fiftieth year, I took the risk. I stepped off. And, yes, the clods hurt my feet – a great deal. But God drew me to himself, and *He began to open my heart.* I suspect my experience was akin to that of one whose experience is recorded in the Bible. Lydia was a worshipper of God – probably one who rationally acknowledged God with prayers and service. Then, during St. Paul's teaching, a miracle happened. We are told that God opened her heart[30]. We are not told exactly what that means, but immediately one can observe the effect on her character – she expresses her love in a unique way.

Though our experiences may vary, the outcomes tend to be very similar. Consider, for example, the experience of another woman, as told by her children;

> *Among the many losses in Mom's life, none was more profound than the loss of her birth mother, whom she never met – her mother having passed away three days after giving birth. It was, therefore, a deeply moving experience for her, at age seventy-three, to discover her mother's grave in a remote country cemetery.*
>
> *The following summer we gathered as a family to place a memorial stone on the unmarked grave and to celebrate the life of the mother and grandmother we never knew.*
>
> *"That experience," Mom writes in her brief memoirs, "filled me with a love so pure and made me realize I had done the best I*

[30] Acts 16:13-15

*could under the circumstances... I still feel a
very deep, deep peace, and love the Lord very
much for what He has done for me."* [31]

When you begin to see with your heart, the whole world changes. God becomes extremely relational and fills your life with joy amidst the pain. Even Scripture takes on new meaning. For me, the beginning of the miracle opened my eyes to see where I was, and where I had come from – and it was not a pleasant sight.

If you are longing for this experience, and are hoping for a quick miracle, as Lydia seemed to experience, do not be fooled. Perhaps it was a quick miracle, but more likely this was the culmination of a long search, prompted by many years of pain. Nor can you settle for a formula to bring about this change – formulas spawn legalism. You see, if you had a formula, you would do it for yourself and end up with counterfeit clutter, not with what God offered. No, God is more mysterious than that. He loves you enough to take you through a journey that will be unique to you, and He will walk with you – just the two of you. That way He can rejoice with you as you rejoice, hold you when you weep, and carry you when you feel you can't go another step.

May I add a word of caution – do not look for a set of seven easy steps on how to experience God. It is my hope that as you read on you will be able to interpret the experiences and commentary into principles that may have application to your life. If you are willing to put that kind

---

[31] An excerpt from "A Tribute to Helen Retzlaff' given by her children at her funeral in 2005. Used with permission.

of thought into this exercise, I am confident you will find it rewarding – and life changing.

My own journey began when my frenetic Christian service took me to its logical conclusion – *Burnout*. My false identity went up in smoke. And I was glad. I had had enough of dealing with 'idiots'. Strange, isn't it, how addiction will burn like a fire in your belly to drive you on, even when you suspect something is seriously amiss. But you don't know how to stop. Then when it happens, you feel tremendous relief. So, when I was invited back onto the treadmill, I declined. I had had enough. I was ready to step off of my comfort pillow, and face reality – though at that point, fortunately I did not know how seriously the clods would bite into my feet.

I enrolled in a counseling program at a seminary – not that I wanted to become a counselor - but I knew I needed counsel. The first semester felt like pure hell. You see, I had taken all the clutter along when I moved - all my self-righteousness, all my arrogance. Consequently, I encountered another batch of 'idiots', who refused to understand me, who ignored me, and left me groveling in self-pity. I was still standing on my comfort pillow and it was becoming increasingly uncomfortable, but I did not know how to get off. I did not trust those who were to mentor me. However, I did respect and trust the head of the department. And though I had little contact with him, he offered hope. Consequently, in spite of the fact that at the end of the first semester I had decided to request a new mentor – one who was not twenty-five years my junior – I made a momentous decision. I did not request a new mentor. Instead I chose to spend the semester opening up my closed mind.

Perhaps I could learn something after all. Seems obvious, doesn't it? But it wasn't. What if these guys were all wrong? When one is used to trusting only in oneself in certain private areas of life, it is not easy to relinquish control – that is the deceptiveness of clutter.

After due consideration, and with some trepidation, I took the risk - to see if I could understand what was going on. But what I needed was not to understand, but to surrender. Surrender to mystery. Surrender to exploring the uncharted territory of my own inner wilderness – a territory I had unwittingly guarded with my very life. Gingerly, I took a step off of my pillow, only to retreat again when the real pain began. There was so much falsehood in my life that needed to be addressed – so many lies that I had come to believe about myself. Risk and retreat. And so much insecurity to deal with, now that the wall I was hiding behind was coming down. Risk and retreat. And so much of it was done in the presence of a dozen or so classmates, as much as thirty years my junior, all wrestling with their own inner demons, under the tutorship of an instructor who didn't think I'd make it. But gradually the comfort of the old pillow dimmed by comparison to the taste of life I was experiencing.

Fortunately, the head of the department offered an evening course for men. I enrolled. Not that I had anything personal to gain, but it was a topic I should know something about after seminary – in case I ever needed to provide leadership for men. It was under his mentorship that I began to explore the truth about me. After each class we were required to journal our feelings, and hand in the journal. One evening the discussion probed our reaction to the Middle East conflict. I sat and listened as the men shared their feelings. After class I wrote, "Here I sit listening to the feelings being expressed around me, and I feel nothing. I am sitting like a bump on a log – totally disconnected." It was likely the first time I had even tried to express what was going on inside of me, and since I wasn't feeling anything, I was sure this journal would spell my failure in the class. It was a difficult journal to hand in – but I resolved to be honest.

The next week, I got the instructor's response. It read, "I am so glad to see that you are so much in touch with where you are at. Congratulations." I sat down and wept. Finally, I felt an acceptance that I had never felt before. Somebody understood. It was a first step in giving me permission to explore a part of me that I had never been aware of – the part that has to do with being, the part called my 'heart'. Among other things, I discovered that emotions are not something you figure out intellectually – emotions are felt. Wow! I had a long way to go, but I had seen the sunrise, and God was beginning to open my heart. What more could one ask? I had *'seen my first gopher'*.

Let me share one story that I believe had a great impact, not only on my heart closing, but also on it opening again years later. When I was a little boy, probably five years old, living in a farming community in southern Alberta, I spent a good deal of time playing by myself. I was really quite creative and made a tractor out of a piece of two-by-four lumber and four shoe polish tins.

A neighbor gal came over, and was so impressed she went home and built one, too. Imagine that, two four-wheel-drive tractors in our community, owned by two farm kids, long before they were even invented for agriculture! That is how my days were spent.

One day my dad asked me to deliver a letter to a neighbor who lived a kilometer down the road. So I took the letter and left. Walking that distance by myself was nothing unusual – though by today's standards it would certainly seem foolhardy. As I approached the house, I realized I had never been there before. The house was old – unpainted. There was no lawn, just weeds and a few tall poplar trees. There were three or four rather battered-looking steps leading up to a small landing, which was about eye-level for me. And the door – I had to look up to see it. For a five-year-old this posed a real dilemma. The landing was small. If I got all the way up there and the door opened to reveal a stranger, my chances of escape appeared to be seriously compromised. So I deliberated how best to get out of the situation - alive. Finally, I decided to lay the envelope on the landing, and leave. It seemed such a creative plan at the time.

When I got home my mom asked me if I had delivered the letter, and I assured her that I had given it to the lady of the house. Then I went out to play. I was out in the yard, playing, when Dad got home some time later. He came over and asked me if I had indeed delivered the letter. I assured him that I had given it to the man of the house. What I had not anticipated was that he may have talked with Mom. It soon became apparent that he had. He challenged my statement with, "But you told Mom that"...

Oops! I was caught! As calmly as I could, I assured him that this was the correct story. I had the distinct feeling that he did not believe me, and I began to brace myself for the worst. In our home, whippings were in place for those caught lying.

He looked down at me for a long moment - I expected him to tell me to go fetch a switch. But he didn't, he just stood looking. And then, without saying a word, he turned about and walked toward the house. He never spoke of it again.

Relieved, I went back to my play totally unaware of the impact this experience would have on my life. It may have been that Dad was doing the most loving thing he could for me under the circumstances, but the subconscious effects on me were traumatic, and long lasting. Had he scooped me up in his arms at that moment, hugged me and apologized for sending me on an errand that was far beyond my years, I expect I would have loved him forever. And it would have reinforced my identity as a person of value, even if I had not performed according to expectation. Shame would not have been given a foothold.

But he didn't. He just walked away, and the subconscious message I absorbed was, "You can't do anything right, can you. You are not even worth whipping." His turning away left the message "You just don't matter!" New lies were reinforced deep in my inner being that day, lies that would progressively guide my life as I got older.

I do not believe that these messages were going through my dad's mind and being projected on to me by his silence. Nor do I believe that I was the one formulating these messages. I do believe that the deceiver waits for just such opportunities, and then whispers the lies into the child's mind. And, to the child's undeveloped logic they seem so reasonable, they sound like truth. This is exacerbated by our design – we were designed to take dominion in conjunction with our Creator. The deception leads us to take control in conjunction with the deceiver. These statements become the best-kept secrets we have. The thrust of my life from here on would be to prove to the world that these statements are not true, all the while having them reinforced in myself, because my failure in performance would prove to me that they were true. Quite a dilemma! I had now entered the arena of shame.

From that time on I needed to prove that I could deliver. At home, that effort never really seemed to pay off, so I compensated by being extremely lazy. But when I began to work in the church, I began to reap the benefits. Suddenly, I awoke. I submit that it was this drive for identity, not some sense of altruism that motivated my service in the church. And how I worked! And how I beat that inner child, when, in my estimation, he failed to deliver, or made some stupid error. For many years it kept me from blossoming in many areas where I could have excelled, had I been free to take the risk.

Another area of my life that was influenced by this experience was my ability to receive a gift. I could give - grudgingly - but I could not receive. During my early university days, I showed a professor a kindness - a rather creative kindness I might add. It was the end of a session of summer school. Several of us spearheaded a movement to give appreciation gifts to our instructors, including some visiting professors, for a job well done. It fell to me to make the presentation to the local professor, who was head of the department.

Knowing of his interest in the then fledgling computer industry – home computers were still many years away - I decided to cover an equipment cart with a large cardboard box, to which I attached a typewriter for a keyboard. I sat inside the box, and propelled the unit into the room, right to where the professor stood. A list of pre-recorded questions slipped out of the side of the box, to which he responded by typing in appropriate answers. At the conclusion, his gift was slipped out as well, and the simulation wheeled itself back out of the room. He was duly impressed.

He offered to fund me through my doctoral studies if I would come work for him in his department. Being unaware of the difficult personal circumstances he found himself in that summer, I did not realize just how much this meant to him. I was later told that the contraption stood in his department for years to come, as a challenge to the students to think creatively. Nor did I realize that this was reportedly the first time in his career that a student had thanked him for his instruction. Nor did it make sense that he should value my creativity. I felt I had manipulated him into making the offer. I declined – it didn't seem right. My wife encouraged me, reminding me that teaching university students had been a dream of mine. She was right. But when you believe that you 'don't matter', there is no way you will let someone make you 'matter'. It violates your sense of integrity to not be required to earn your keep. Such is the strength of childhood deceptions.

So the little boy was controlling my adult life. Unwittingly, I hated him for it, and beat him often – but beating never caused him to respond in love.

Then I discovered that if I wanted God to open my heart, I had to begin to open my heart to the little boy. I had no idea how hard that would be. Somehow the lies I had learned when I failed to deliver the letter had to be addressed. It is at that very point that repentance offered a pathway back on the journey toward wholeness. To do this, I visualized the experience again, and tried to make contact with a little boy who didn't trust me – why should he, after the many beatings that I had given him? At first, all I could do was tell him that the experience was not his fault - his dad had been expecting too much from him. It was a rational beginning to an emotional issue. Then I volunteered to take him by the hand, and we delivered the letter together. Good move, but we were still performing. I must admit it was some time before I could throw my arms around him, give him a kiss, and say, "You are valuable – you matter to me. Let's go play together. I love you." And some time later yet, till he could respond. But when he became liberated to accept love, then I, too, could begin to accept love. Amazingly, the need to perform lost its grip. And right and wrong didn't matter anymore. The truth was that God was offering me grace - a gift I was now open to receive, giving me something that I could revel in, and even extend to others. So God, in his mercy, began cutting through the clutter, opening my heart, and revealing the sunrise – and that's enough for me. Sure beats standing on a pile of dried horse manure trying to control the world.

Do I still see 'idiots'? Very rarely I do, and then only momentarily. Instead I see little boys and girls, dressed in adult bodies, running to and fro, trying to get some sense of value by performing, when they do not know how to receive love. And I weep.

If, on reflecting on my story, you too have seen a little child - lonely, abandoned, looking for someone to care – I encourage you to open your heart to him/her. That child has been waiting many years for someone to love it and liberate it from the lies it believes. And who knows? You might just find a new freedom yourself. It is interesting in this regard, to contemplate the words of Jesus,

> *"Assuredly, I say to you, unless you are converted and become as little children, you will by no means enter the kingdom of heaven. Therefore whoever humbles himself as this little child is the greatest in the kingdom of heaven. Whoever receives one little child like this in My name receives Me."*
> (Matthew 18:3-5)

I must, however, offer a word of caution. We were created to take dominion in conjunction with our Creator. None-the-less, we are schooled in the 'Right vs. Wrong' paradigm from birth. I believe this is part of the deceiver's strategy. So our God-given ability to take dominion gets perverted into a strategy to take control to protect our 'self'. If we have a sin nature, that is what I suggest it is – a perversion of our God-given gift to take dominion. In short, we are introduced to spiritual battle at a very early age – not fighting the deceiver, but being deceived, and thinking we are right. And the deceiver well knows that if we can be shamed, and bullied into hiding, we will never receive the love we are being offered.

> *'He who receives nothing, has nothing to return'*[32]

Hence, when we begin to do the hard work of reclaiming our 'self', we are in spiritual battle – regardless of whether we have knowledge of God or not. I have witnessed men and women weeping for the little inner child as they see its pain, and then celebrating as they connect lovingly again. But I have also witnessed some closing up again after a period of time if they do not access adequate support.

> *'The stitch is lost, unless the thread is knotted.'*[33]

One day Jesus told this most intriguing story,

> *"When an unclean spirit goes out of a man, he goes through dry places, seeking rest; and finding none, he says, 'I will return to my house from which I came.' "And when he comes, he finds it swept and put in order. "Then he goes and takes with him seven other spirits more wicked than himself, and they*

---

[32] German Proverb
[33] Italian Proverb

enter and dwell there; and the last state of that
man is worse than the first." (Luke 11:24-26)

I do not claim to know just what that story means, but I have observed a similar pattern for those who reconnect with the inner child, and then do not carry on in celebration. Since it is a spiritual battle, it may be that this story does apply. At any rate, it seems reasonable to me, that if it were Jesus who facilitated the reconnection with the inner child (I am convinced it was not the deceiver), then I would want him resident to facilitate the relationship and avoid further deceit. He is waiting for your permission to be your friend and protector, but an invitation would be fitting. Do not be surprised to find amazing things happening in your life as you begin to love.

As I began to love, I recognized others who were not part of the 'Christian religion' crowd. Somehow, in spite of the deception, they love, and they are compassionate. These are people who do not spend time performing. They rarely appear on the public stage. They are rarely found in administration. They don't need to be. Jesus has met their emptiness. He has filled their hearts with love. They operate in the background, serving their God with joy, picking up those hurt in the battle, being salt in a bland world. These are the ones whose heart God has opened – opened to receive his love, opened to love others, opened to receive confirmation of their identity in Him, and opened to accept the peace and rest promised to the people of God. But they are not in the majority.

In summary, then, what does it mean to have one's heart opened? Basically, I believe, the experience is akin to that of a young eaglet learning to fly. While it was growing in the nest, I presume it developed an outlook on life that involved having its daily needs met, and enjoying the warmth and safety of the nest. If an eagle can think rationally, it would likely develop a philosophy of life based on that experience. It may even involve a pecking order in the nest, based on the powerful controlling, even killing, the less powerful. That system works for a while. But there comes a time when the eaglet, for its own good, must leave the nest - or die. But if it jumps, it had better soar, even if it has never soared before. So leaving the security of the nest can be pretty scary – parents have been observed starving the youngster, and then hovering just out of reach with a fresh kill to entice the young eaglet.[34] But if it flies, a whole new life opens up before it, and a whole new view of the world, and a whole new freedom. And though it may take an eaglet several months to learn to appreciate that view, and more time till it learns how to hunt, a new life has begun.

> "But those who wait on the LORD
> Shall renew their strength;
> They shall mount up with wings like eagles,
> They shall run and not be weary,
> They shall walk and not faint." (Isaiah 40:31)

That was my experience. Suddenly the Scriptures took on a whole new meaning, as I understood them from

---

[34]First Flights, http://baldeagleinfo.com/eagle/eagle4.html

a relational perspective, rather than a rational one. Almost as though I were seeing a sunrise, and a whole new day were dawning. Romeo captured the thought well in his conversation with Juliet on the balcony when he said:[35]

> ...look, love, what envious streaks
> Do lace the severing clouds in yonder east:
> Night's candles are burnt out, and jocund day
> Stands tiptoe on the misty mountain tops.
> I must be gone and live, or stay and die.

Those were my feelings when God began to open my heart. And indeed, there is a need to grow with the experience, or die. I cannot predict what the experience will be like for you should you decide to embrace it, but when it happens, you will begin to live in a totally new paradigm.

> The wind blew hot against my face
> As I ran to the meadow for a change of pace;
> Here in the meadow the wind blew free,
> The grasses swayed like the waves of the sea.
>
> As I stood there alone my eyes did fall
> On a dandelion standing so proud and tall.
> I viewed it, and then I said with a grin,
> "Out on my lawn you'd look ugly as sin!"
>
> But here in the meadow you seem to belong,
> With all your golden, and white-haired throng.
> Here in the meadow is just the place

---

[35] http://shakespeare.mit.edu/romeo_juliet/romeo_juliet.3.3.html

Where even you can light up a face.

With the sky so blue, and the sun so warm,
Somewhere in the meadow, peace must
have been born.
Oh, how I longed for this peace on earth
That all could know their own self worth.

I bowed my head and I prayed in reflection
"Dear God, give me, in this world of perfection
A heart, that would know no colour nor creed,
That each may be known by one's merit and deed"[36]

Let me sum up with a thumbnail sketch that links the process of moving toward authenticity with a corresponding promise as found in the Beatitudes.[37]

THE PROCESS	THE PROMISE
1. Facing our Denial: Giving up the mask	*Blessed are the poor in spirit for theirs is the kingdom of heaven.*
2. Facing our Pain: Learning to receive	*Blessed are those who mourn for they will be comforted.*
3. Facing our Fears: Giving up destructiveness	*Blessed are the meek for they will inherit the earth.*
4. Facing our Longings: Allowing God to meet our needs	*Blessed are those who hunger and thirst for righteousness for they will be filled.*

---

[36] *The Meadow,* an unpublished poem by the late Helen Retzlaff (1928-2005) Used with permission
[37] Matthew 5:3-13

5. Giving up Control: Learning to forgive	*Blessed are the merciful for they will be shown mercy.*
6. Clarifying our Motives: Becoming authentic	*Blessed are the pure in heart for they will see God.*
7. Listening Beneath Words: Learning to understand	*Blessed are the peacemakers for they will be called sons of God.*
8. Welcoming Adversity: Becoming free to love	*Blessed are those who are persecuted because of righteousness for theirs is the Kingdom of Heaven.*
9. Seeing as God Sees: Celebrating relationship with God	*Blessed are you when they revile and persecute you, and say all kinds of evil against you falsely for My sake.*

"Rejoice and be exceedingly glad, for great is your reward in heaven, for so they persecuted the prophets who were before you."

CHAPTER FIVE
Fostering True Identity

*The promise of yesterday is
that there will be a tomorrow.*

> *"...No one puts new wine into old
> wineskins; or else the new wine will
> burst the wineskins and be spilled, and
> the wineskins will be ruined. "But new
> wine must be put into new wineskins,
> and both are preserved. "And no one,
> having drunk old wine, immediately
> desires new; for he says, 'The old is
> better.'"* (Luke 5:37-39)

In ancient times wine was stored in goatskins. As the
grape juice fermented, it would expand and stretch the
skin. With time, the skin would become less resilient,
which did not pose a problem because the contents had
stabilized. Jesus was explaining to his listeners that when
faith is no longer stretching, it can be contained in a rather
stiff theology – in this case, a legalistic theology defined by
right and wrong.

However, he goes on to say that if a vibrant faith is
contained in a stiff theology, it will burst that way of
thinking, and because the new faith lacks a doctrinal base,
both will be lost. Hence, he suggests if one's faith is

expanding and growing, it is important to contain it within a more flexible theology that will allow for the preservation of both. In short, those growing in their faith may wish to re-examine their theological base, to see if it is compatible with a growing faith.

But Jesus adds a word of caution – most people will be more comfortable with what has been, than with what could be. If what has been, has been confined within a paradigm of 'Right vs. Wrong', the new will immediately be branded as wrong because it does not feel comfortable. Stretching only brings comfort if it happens within certain defined limits.

As God began to open my heart, I could begin to see a broader picture of the love of God. He wanted to fill me with the new wine of his spirit that would ferment and expand within me. But first, he had to make sure the container was flexible enough to contain the blessing so that nothing would be lost - hence, the painful process of replacing the old stiff skin.

In this chapter I invite you to explore a new way of thinking that is flexible enough to expand with expanding faith, and provides for a new level of intimacy with God and with mankind. For some, it will be most uncomfortable, while others will welcome it as a theological perspective that not only allows the power of God to flow and expand, but that encourages deep, meaningful relationship. Whatever your persuasion, may this provide the incentive for you to study the Scripture for yourself, so you may own your own faith.

The gospel-writer, John, said,

*And the Word became flesh and dwelt among
us, and we beheld His glory, the glory as of
the only begotten of the Father, full of grace
and truth.* (John 1:14)

When the heart opens to grace and truth, a whole
new philosophy of life unfolds before us. A new
worldview emerges.

*For the law was given through Moses, but
grace and truth came through Jesus Christ.*
(John 1:17)

It is the radical concept of 'Grace with Truth' that
Jesus introduced when he came to free humanity from the
deception that had engulfed it. St. Paul reinforces this
thought when he says, *"Stand fast therefore in the liberty by
which Christ has made us free, and do not be entangled again
with a yoke of bondage."* (Galatians 5:1)

One of the major differences between the two
paradigms, I would suggest, is that Christian *religion* is
based on right versus wrong, which creates a closed mind;
Christian *faith* is based on grace and truth, which creates
an open heart. Not that one is no longer aware of right and
wrong - even Adam and Eve in the garden must have
noticed the species of tree called 'The Knowledge of Good
and Evil' growing amidst the other trees of the garden. But
it did not concern them. They did not base their lives on
the consumption of its fruit. They simply lived with it.
Their lives revolved around communion with 'Him who is
the Truth', and who offers grace to all. Living in this

paradigm involves getting used to letting God be God – which means one must get used to living with mystery.

Another difference could be illustrated by my recent interaction with an auto mechanic. With respect to a certain customer, he said, "I just get that guy's car fixed, and it works fine in the shop, but all he needs to do is take the car home, and within a day or two he will make the problem reoccur." According to this mechanic, his diagnosis of the problem was always right, and the customer was at fault if the problem was not repaired. Had he lived with a 'Grace with Truth' worldview, the mechanic might have called the customer and admitted that if the problem reoccurred, perhaps his diagnosis had been faulty, and he would be willing to explore further.

A third major difference is the attitude that each creates as we contemplate people – those made in the image and likeness of the Creator. Suppose, for example, you saw a young prostitute working the street, and you took the time to actually reflect on her situation. Would you see a sinner 'doing her thing'? Or would you see a holy one, who has been deceived into believing that she has no value, other than to be a slave to another's pleasure? For which would you weep? To which would you extend your heart?

IS IT POSSIBLE THAT GOD CREATED ME HOLY AND PURPOSEFUL?

Are my beliefs, about how I was introduced to sin, significant? I hesitate to say 'became a sinner' since I find nowhere that Jesus ever called anyone a sinner to his face as he talked with them. He would, however, respond in kind. If someone accused him of eating with sinners, he would respond by saying that it was sinners he came to save. In short, he spoke to people in their own language. The only exception I find is when he was being arrested. He told his disciples that he was falling into the hands of sinners – and here I suspect he was referring, not to the army about to seize him, but to the broader context of sinful humanity. If Jesus was careful not to address people as sinners, I suggest we would be wise to use the term with discretion as well.

About the same time that Tertullian was formulating his theory on sin in Carthage, another view was being suggested in Alexandria. A scholar by the name of Clement, and his protégé, Origen, suggested that the origin of the soul happens simultaneously with the formation of the body, and that all people are born with a free will and then choose to sin. This view came to be accepted by the Christian churches in the eastern half of the Roman Empire. It is interesting to note that the eastern empire outlasted the west by some thousand years. One wonders if this may have been influenced by their belief system. It is also intriguing that John, the author of the Revelation, only mentions churches in Asia Minor as he addresses the churches of the day.

Following are some Scripture verses, which may have influenced Origen's view in regards to the human condition at birth.[38] Notice the kind of identity statements

---

[38] For a fuller list of Scripture references refer to: <u>Over One Hundred Texts From the Bible That Show That Babies Are Born Innocent and Without Sin </u>by A.T. Overstreet

God makes when he is introducing the birth of the following babies. When the word of the Lord came to Jeremiah, this is what he heard:

> "Before I formed you in the womb I knew you;
> Before you were born I sanctified you;
> I ordained you a prophet to the nations."
> (Jeremiah 1:5)

When the angel appeared to Manoah's wife regarding the birth of Sampson, this is the message she heard:

> "For behold, you shall conceive and bear a son. And no razor shall come upon his head, for the child shall be a Nazirite[39] to God from the womb; and he shall begin to deliver Israel out of the hand of the Philistines." (Judges 13:5)

When the angel appeared to Zacharias in the temple with a message regarding the birth of his son John, later known as the Baptizer, Zacharias heard;

> "For he will be great in the sight of the Lord, and shall drink neither wine nor strong drink. He will also be filled with the Holy Spirit, even from his mother's womb." (Luke 1:15)

And when the angel appeared to Mary regarding the birth of Jesus, his message was,

> *"The Holy Spirit will come upon you, and the power of the Highest will overshadow you; therefore, also, that Holy One who is to be born will be called the Son of God."* (Luke 1:35)

Isaiah speaks the following words;

> *"And now the LORD says,*
> *Who formed Me from the womb to be*
> *His Servant, to bring Jacob back to Him"*
> (Isaiah 49:5)

Even St. Paul suggests that God had set him apart for a purpose even while he was in his mother's womb.[40]

Since the Scriptures make a point of naming examples of those whom God created as holy infants, would it not seem reasonable to suggest there should also be named examples of those who were born a sinner, if there were any? My search has not found any. The closest example would be Ishmael, who was predicted to be a wild donkey of a man, not a sinner.

One would expect that if the principle were true, current examples would reinforce it. Can we find examples of children who have known Jesus since birth, even if they had never received any religious training?

---

[40] Galatians 1:15-16 But when it pleased God, who separated me from my mother's womb and called *me* through His grace, to reveal His Son in me, that I might preach Him among the Gentiles ...

When Dr. Diane Komp started her career as a pediatric cancer specialist, she described herself as somewhere between agnostic and atheist. Through her experiences at the bedside of many dying children, she returned to a belief in God, and recognized the reality of God's love. The fact that children undergoing the pain and suffering of terminal illness knew Jesus in spite of not having had religious training served as powerful evidence to the existence of God. She says,

> *"The ways of children are a deep mystery. Children hold the key to unlocking life's greatest mysteries... When the clever are really intelligent, they look to children for answers."[41]*

Another interesting example is the child prodigy, Akiane Kramarik. Says her mother,

> *"Our family never talked about religion, never prayed together, and never went to any church. I had been raised as an atheist in Lithuania, and Markus had been raised in an environment not conducive to spiritual growth. The children did not watch television, had never been out of our sight, and were home schooled; therefore, we were certain that no one else could have influenced Akiane's sudden and detailed descriptions of an invisible realm. We can't remember the*

---

[41] Komp, Diane, <u>A Window to Heaven</u>, (Grand Rapids, Zondervan, 1992) pp. 48-49

78

exact month, but one morning when Akiane was four, she began sharing her visions of heaven with us. "Today I met God," Akiane whispered to me one morning".[42] ... "Akiane is convinced that the greatest gift we could give to God, who has everything and does not need anything except our love, is for us to love one another and walk in faith, day by day, hour by hour. Now we, as her parents, believe that too. For by trusting Akiane and by listening to her messages, which were divinely inspired yet masked with childish laughter, we were rewarded with one of the greatest gifts of all: faith."[43]

Indeed, it has been my privilege to know one, who, as a small child suffered horrendous abuse at the hands of adults. Following such episodes, she would retire to a place of solitude, to be comforted by her friend – Jesus. She had no religious training or association. She just knew him – always knew him. Why should we be amazed that Jesus really does love little children – and that they return his love? After all, he said,

"Let the little children come to Me, and do not forbid them; for of such is the kingdom of God. Assuredly, I say to you, whoever does not receive the kingdom of God as a little child will by no means enter it." (Mark 10:14-15)

[42] Akiane and Foreli Kramarik, <u>Akiane: Her Life, Her Art, Her Poetry</u> (Nashville; W Publishing Group, 2006) p. 7
[43] ibid, p. 40

Even St. Paul, who is often quoted as favoring the view that all were born sinners, makes statements that may bring this view into question. Consider, for example, the following thought:

> *"I was alive once without the law, but when the commandment came, sin revived and I died."* (Romans 7:9)

Is he not affirming his belief that in his childhood he was spiritually alive, but when he chose to subscribe to the law, he died?

IF WE WERE BORN HOLY, AT WHAT AGE DO WE BECOME ACCOUNTABLE?

Moses, the one credited with writing the first five books of the Old Testament, gives us a hint. In Genesis he give us an account of the creation of the universe and all its inhabitants. Then he introduces the concept that sin arises when one trusts the 'Knowledge of Good and Evil' rather than God for sustenance. He goes on to describe how a man and a woman fell prey to deception, gained intimate knowledge of good and evil, and died. In Deuteronomy he retells the story, with a twist. Now the Israelite nation is faced with entering the Promised Land, and again must decide whether to follow God, or let their own knowledge of good and evil determine their course. Again, they succumb to the deception, and are doomed for discharge from the garden, but God makes an exception. Moses writes,

*"Moreover your little ones and your children,
who you say will be victims, who today have
no knowledge of good and evil, they shall go
in there; to them I will give it, and they shall
possess it."* (Deuteronomy 1:39)

Moses is mentioning a group to be excluded from
punishment – the children and little ones who have no
knowledge of good and evil. As with Adam and Eve, the
implication is that without this knowledge they have not
sinned. Thus Moses suggests that children are born sinless.
So how old were these children who had not yet sinned?
The answer is found in the previous book. Again Moses is
speaking for God,

*"The carcasses of you who have complained
against Me shall fall in this wilderness, all of
you who were numbered, according to your
entire number, from twenty years old and
above."* (Numbers 14:29)

One could conclude that the age of accountability
for the Israelite children of that day was twenty –
according to God, that is.

When Jesus was instructing the Pharisees and
teachers of the law about his mission, he told them a story –
generally known as the story of the prodigal son. He said:

*"A certain man had two sons. 12"And the
younger of them said to his father, 'Father,
give me the portion of goods that falls to me.'
So he divided to them his livelihood. 13"And*

not many days after, the younger son gathered all together, journeyed to a far country, and there wasted his possessions with prodigal living." (Luke 15:11-32)

Note the maturity of the young man when he broke relationship with his father. Leaving his childhood home was the deliberate choice of a young man. In fact, it was done at great risk, since asking for inheritance before one's parent died was akin to a death wish on the parent – and was punishable by death. Note also that he was resident in his father's house, not the house of an enemy. If you read the whole story, you will also note that he comes back to live at his father's house again, wanting to come as a servant (Right vs. Wrong Paradigm*)*. The father, however, lives in another paradigm (Grace with Truth) and welcomes him back as a son. Father and son have been *reconciled*. The theme of the story speaks eloquently of a lad who began life in relationship with his father, and then breaks that relationship when he is old enough to make that choice, only to return, again by choice, and accept grace.

IS THERE A PROCESS THAT LEADS ME INTO SIN?

Basically the question is, "How do I become inducted into the paradigm of 'Right vs. Wrong'? St. Paul expresses his concern to the Corinthian church:

> *"But I fear, lest somehow, as the serpent deceived Eve by his craftiness, so your minds*

*may be corrupted from the simplicity that is
in Christ."* (2 Corinthians 11:3)

Here St. Paul suggests that his listeners had the
potential of being deceived by an external force – a
deception that will corrupt minds. John, the Revelator,
affirms who is causing the deception,

> *"So the great dragon was cast out, that serpent
> of old, called the Devil and Satan, who deceives
> the whole world..."* (Revelation 12:9)

Might I suggest that when a child is born, the
parents unwittingly plant a 'Tree of the Knowledge of
Good and Evil' beside the cradle. Then the teaching begins:
this is good, this is evil, this is right, this is wrong. What
would happen if our concentration changed to: Here is
truth, here is truth, here is truth, and when you don't get
it, I extend grace? The truth does not exclude love,
compassion, discipline, mentoring. But think of the effects
on children if our concentration were celebrating their
holiness, and moving toward preserving it, rather than
trying to punish them for their perceived sinfulness. And
think of the influence on parenting if you believed that the
infant you held in your arms were holy rather than sinful.

I FACE INIQUITY – I TRANSGRESS – I SIN

You may have noticed that the Scriptures include
the words 'iniquity' and 'transgression' in context with sin.
For the inquirer who asks why, a standard answer is,

"Those are just different adjectives the writers used lest you get bored hearing the word sin over and over."

Elmer Martens, on the other hand, suggests the trio of words; iniquity, transgression, and sin, "when used in combination is intended to convey every possible way of wrong-doing."[44] Each has a unique meaning. He sees iniquity as *a loss of transparency*, transgression as *a breakdown of trust,* and sin as *a failure in relationship*. With that in mind, let us examine the behavior of Adam and Eve in the Garden. When the serpent confronted Eve regarding eating fruit, she quoted God as having said, 'You shall not eat it, nor shall you touch it, lest you die.' It would appear that Eve may not have been totally transparent at this moment, a fact that was confirmed when we observe that she 'saw that the tree *was* good for food, that it *was* pleasant to the eyes, and a tree desirable to make *one* wise.' She may have appeared to be listening to God, but in her mind she was considering something else. Then she "took of its fruit.' She was preparing to trust her own judgment rather than God's suggestion – her trust in God was breaking down. Then she ate, and discovered her relationship with God had failed – she had sinned. She ran off and hid, after getting her partner involved.

It is important to note that, at its base, sin has more to do with attitude than with behavior. The attitude finds expression in action. Jesus said,

> *"You have heard that it was said to those of old, 'You shall not commit adultery.' "But I*

[44] Martens, Elmer, <u>God's Design: A Focus on Old Testament Theology,</u> Grand Rapids: Baker Book House, 1990, p50

say to you that whoever looks at a woman to lust for her has already committed adultery with her in his heart." (Matthew 5:27-28)

It is breaking relationship with God, saying in effect, "God, I don't need you. I can do this on my own, thank you very much!" It is the end result of a process that begins with a lack of transparency, and moves to lack of trust.

We can see the same process in another event recorded in the book of 2Samuel 11. King David had not gone to war – his normal spring adventure - so he needed an ego fix. He saw a woman bathing, and began to ask questions. Though he may have appeared to need this information as king, that was not his intent – he was no longer transparent. He had an inner emptiness, and rather than trust God to fill his need, he began to explore a way to do it himself. He invited the woman to his apartment – his trust in his God was rapidly fading. He found his solution in copulation – he sinned. Copulation was merely the symptom of his sin. He had broken relationship with his God. Later he admits to God, "Against you only have I sinned." (Psalm 51:4) And be sure of this: when we sin, others will be hurt and violated in the crossfire.

Recorded in Luke 15, we find three stories of things lost. A sheep, perhaps involved in eating and walking as she ate, suddenly became aware that the relationship with her shepherd had been lost. A coin, through lack of care on the part of its steward, became lost. A young man made a conscious decision to leave home and break relationship. In the first two cases, the owner went out searching for the lost object. In the third, the father respected the choice of his son and waited at the door, knowing his love would draw him back when things got tough. In all of these cases, being lost had to do with being separated from a caregiver – a situation that was rectified through restoration.

SUBSCRIBING TO A *RIGHT VS. WRONG* PARADIGM KILLS ME

When we understand what is right and what is wrong, and let this become the guiding principle in our lives, we no longer need God. *We have become god.* But, since this violates the relationship for which we were created, our true self, dies, and all that is left is a counterfeit. St. Paul suggests;

> *"I was alive once without the law, but when the commandment came, sin revived and I died."* (Romans 7:9)

I REAP PAINFUL CONSEQUENCES; I AM WOUNDED; I LONG FOR GOD

Both the Old and New Testaments are replete with stories of people who have suffered painful consequences for their sin. The Psalmist says,

> *When I kept silent, my bones grew old*
> *Through my groaning all the day long.*
> *For day and night Your hand was heavy upon me;*
> *My vitality was turned into the drought of*
> *summer. Selah.*

I acknowledged my sin to You,
And my iniquity I have not hidden.
I said, "I will confess my transgressions to the
    LORD,"
And You forgave the iniquity of my sin. Selah.
(Psalm 32:3-5)

Recognizing and facing our sin, rather than denying it, opens our eyes to the fact that our own efforts are inadequate - we need divine help. Humility opens the door. Jesus said,

> *"Blessed are the poor in spirit, for theirs is*
> *the kingdom of heaven."* (Matthew 5:3)

HOW IS RELATIONSHIP RESTORED?

Jesus said, *"No one can come to Me unless the Father who sent Me draws him; and I will raise him up at the last day. It is written in the prophets, 'And they shall all be taught by God.' Therefore everyone who has heard and learned from the Father comes to Me."* (John 6:44-45)

A common boast among some who practice the Christian religion is to talk of how many people they 'won to the Lord'. Somehow that doesn't seem to line up with Jesus' teaching. Imagine a mid-wife talking about how many babies she had birthed, when indeed she had only been present to assist as others birthed them. For the faith-based Christian, a more biblical approach would be to celebrate the honor of having been present while the Holy Spirit birthed those whom the Father had drawn.

But a larger question arises. How do I receive the Father's love? That is a mystery. I have outlined my experience in moving toward love in a previous chapter. However, allow me to explore another aspect of receiving love.

Christian religion tends to see the words 'heart' and 'head' as synonyms for the same concept. It is a belief system that focuses on rational logic, rather than the unpredictability of emotion. This is evidenced in the struggle to rationally define love, as noted earlier. When we have no awareness of our emotional nature, defining love becomes a rather clinical exercise. The practice of love also becomes clinical, arising out of a need to do one's duty to God. The attitude can often be encapsulated in, "I'll love you even if it kills me!" Or to follow up on the speaker mentioned at the end of chapter three, "Kick me in the pants and I will love you." Hence, love is stripped of all emotion and mystery, and is transformed into co-dependence.

Unfortunately, this philosophy has influenced the modern-speech translators of the Scriptures as well. In our modern wisdom the words 'bowel', 'spleen', and 'kidney' from the original writings have been removed from their former association with love. Hence it is rather unusual but refreshing to hear journalists again begin to describe experience as involving the head, heart, and gut.

Throughout the original New Testament writings not only the words 'mind' and 'heart' frequently appear, but also the word 'bowels' and 'spleen'. In the Old Testament writings, the word 'mind' does not appear, - relationships were defined by the words; 'heart', 'bowels', and 'kidneys'. Though there is mystery in how these all relate, modern scientific research is proving the ancient ideas to be valid – each is significant.

Dr. Aiko Hormon, research scientist specializing in 'Artificial Intelligence and the Brain', was one of the first Christian researches to suggest we actually have three centers of intelligence in our bodies – a head brain, a heart brain, and a gut brain.[45] I suspect these could correspond to; a dominant cognitive center, an intuitive center, and a motivational center. For a hypothetical model refer to figure 5-1.

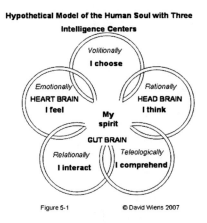

Figure 5-1   © David Wiens 2007

A study of these three brains in the Scripture would suggest that each performs a rather specialized and unique function in our relationships.[46] Each appears to be neutral – hence the mind can be reprobate, renewed, enlightened, or darkened, to name a few. The heart can be pure, sincere, hardened, or deceitful. The gut can be pressed for room or restricted, affectionate, shut up, or flowing with living

---

[45] www.dr-aiko.com/
[46] For selected lists of Scriptures referring to the head, heart, and gut, see Appendix One, should you wish to draw your own conclusions.

waters. Where the head and the heart appear to be more involved in decision-making, the gut appears to be more of a receptacle that contains that which defines what we are all about. Reflect on some of the common terms about the gut: to have guts, gut instinct, intestinal fortitude, raw gut courage, gut feeling, kicked in the gut, hate your guts, gut wrenching – all speak of something deep within us.

Might I suggest that when I am emotionally wounded, I will repress my feelings, because that is safer than living with the deep shame of the negative messages I believe about my self. As my gut brain becomes restricted, I feel the emptiness within, but having no way to address it, I massage my soul by succumbing to addictions. Hence, if I am intellectually gifted, I will communicate rationally in order to feel some sense of control.

However, when I encounter someone whom I can trust, I begin to open up emotionally. If my trust was well placed, and I make a rational choice to begin to listen to the heart, I am given the opportunity to begin to trust my emotions. I begin to counter the lies I have believed about myself, and I begin to discover who I really am. I believe that as this process progresses, a trust grows between the head brain and the heart brain. As the head brain begins to understand the heart brain, the heart brain begins to feel acceptance, and the head brain begins to sense that it is being understood. This begins to foster a sense of significance and belonging in the gut brain, allowing it to cause the heart to feel loved, and the head to feel understood. In short, the capacities are beginning to work together as they were designed to do. If the individual begins to trust his/her Creator, there will be a communication between the spirit within and the Spirit of God confirming that a father/child relationship exists,[47] further intensifying significance and belonging.

When the gut brain is expanded and fulfilled, decision-making will proceed on two fronts[48]. From a deep sense of relational belonging, and a deep sense of emotional acceptance, the individual will know by intuition what the decision is. From a deep sense of teleological significance, and a rational sense of understanding and being understood, the individual will cognitively confirm the intuitive decision. The soul will operate in unity – there will be need for neither defensiveness nor waffling. The spirit will be at peace, and the individual will experience a deep sense of serenity.

Let me elaborate on how I experienced this inter-relationship. I enrolled in seminary with the intent of acquiring more knowledge. But trying to figure out what was happening in the counseling department just resulted in confusion. Before I could move ahead, I needed to open my mind to the possibility that something was going on that I did not understand. I needed to face mystery. At that point I did not trust God in this matter, but because I had some confidence in the department head, I made a decision to do some exploration. In short, my mind seemed to give my heart some permission to exist, separate from the mind. When my heart felt the thrill of being taken seriously, all manner of emotional pain began to emerge – pain that required a good deal of grieving. As this was processed and

---

[47] Romans 8:16 The Spirit Himself bears witness with our spirit that we are children of God,

[48] For a review of this concept, see Chapter Two, Exploring Identity

dealt with, the heart began to feel confident in its own right. It would survive. The heart, then, gave the mind permission to be renewed, as St. Paul suggests, *"be renewed in the spirit of your mind"* (Ephesians 4:23). Because I was beginning to trust God, the mind opened to explore even more mystery.

I was beginning to discover, in my mind and in my heart, positive truth about myself as God revealed it to me. I believe that this opened the door for the truths to be recorded deep within me – in my gut, if you wish. There they have become part of my way of life. The turmoil in my gut subsided. My relationship with my Heavenly Father took on a whole new meaning. I suspect that it is the properly filled gut that produces the deep assurance of the value of our own personhood. There, Jesus affirms my identity.

I suspect 'gut' also describes the residence of the Holy Spirit in the sense that from here emanates the fruit of the Spirit – love, joy, peace, patience, gentleness, goodness, faith, meekness, self-control. Indeed, I would suggest that these are deeper than emotions – they are motivations from the very gut. It becomes a solid, stabilizing force within. I suggest this is what St. Paul had in mind when he said,

> *"And do not be drunk with wine, in which is dissipation; but be filled with the Spirit, speaking to one another in psalms and hymns and spiritual songs, singing and making melody in your heart to the Lord, giving thanks always for all things to God the Father in the name of our Lord Jesus*

Christ, submitting to one another in the fear
of God." (Ephesians 5:18-21)

By contrast, when the heart is closed, the gut may well be 'restricted' and clamor to be satisfied. This 'restriction'[49], I would suggest, is felt as emotional hunger that may be quieted temporarily with wine according to St. Paul. It may well be that this hunger is the source of all addiction, as people try all manner of pleasures to fill their emptiness. St. Paul in his letter to the Galatians lists a few - sexual immorality, impurity and debauchery, idolatry and witchcraft, hatred, discord, jealously, fits of rage, selfish ambition, dissensions, factions and envy, drunkenness, orgies and the like. Jesus said,

> *But those things which proceed out of the*
> *mouth, come forth from the heart; and they*
> *defile the man. For out of the heart proceed evil*
> *thoughts, murders, adulteries, fornications,*
> *thefts, false witness, blasphemies.* (Matthew
> 15:18-19)

My take on the above is that when the heart is closed and the gut is restricted, the emotional hunger drives one to all types of manipulations in an effort to satisfy the hunger.

While the gut appears to be associated with actions arising out of how we are filled, the heart is involved with emotion – in all likelihood stimulated directly from the gut. If, while my gut is filled with gentleness, I am

---

[49] St Paul's definition in 2Corinthians 6:12

approached by someone needing help I will likely feel compassion. If my gut is restricted, I will likely respond with impatience or contempt, or I will manipulate by using the situation to offer help so I can feel good about myself. The heart also is involved in attitude, motivation, disposition, understanding, and courage. St. Paul goes so far as to suggest the heart is essential for righteousness.[50] Some of these characteristics are also associated with the mind, but at a very much more superficial level. Emotional intelligence offers a much deeper and more complete view of life than does rational intelligence alone. Just as our physical depth perception is based on looking with two eyes, so restoring healthy relaltionship requires both emotional insight and intellectual intelligence.

I realize the above process may appear to be rather clinical. I must admit, however, that while I was in the early stages of this process, I did not see any pattern – just a lot of confusion. It is in retrospect, with the advantage of time, that one not only sees pattern in the process, but one truly begins to enjoy its results.

> *"Blessed are those who mourn, for they shall be comforted."* (Matthew 5:4)

JESUS RESTORES ME – MY 'SELF' IS RESURRECTED

A number of years ago, I was in a classroom where the professor was telling the biblical story of how a young

---

[50] Romans 10:10 For with the heart one believes unto righteousness, and with the mouth confession is made unto salvation.

man (the prodigal son) had gathered his goods and left home.[51] When he regained his senses in the pigpen, he decided to go back to his father to be a servant. As the professor spoke of the loving father's response, I saw a picture in my mind – perhaps a vision – of a small boy standing in the driveway as the father approached. The boy's head was bowed in shame, his shoulders slouched, his hands in his pockets, and he was scuffing the gravel with his foot. My first response was, "Who is that?" He reminded me of a little boy who had failed to deliver a letter many years before, and was, even now, waiting for condemnation. And indeed, upon reflection, that is exactly what I was. And though the father was inviting me to a banquet, I had come home to be a servant – a person who earns his keep, but never celebrates because it would violate the integrity of the vow he made. When I saw this, I repented, *"Father, I'm sorry for insisting on being the servant. Forgive me. I want to be your son again. I want the ring, the robe, and the sandals. Open my heart to celebrate with you."*

> *A lost and lonely boy*
> *A boy not knowing where to go or what to do*
> *Just standing by the roadside of life*
> *His hands in his pockets,*
> *For there is no other place for them*
> *Head hung low,*
> *Wondering about life…*
> *He just stands there kicking up loose stones*
> *Building small ditches in the dust with his foot*
> *Hat brim hung low over his eyes*

---

[51] Luke 15:11-24

His shoulders hung in despair
A little boy scared to grow up
Scared because he wonders where he'll fit in,
Even though he doesn't seem to now
A little boy
Forever afraid to grow up[52]

Not too long after that, our family met at the home of one of our children. Over dinner I recounted the story. I had no sooner mentioned 'little boy' when one of my adult sons jumped to his feet, full of questions; "Was the boy's head bowed? Was his cap pulled over his eyes? Were his shoulders slouched? Were his hands in his pockets? Was he scuffing the gravel with the big toe on his right foot?" When I answered yes to each of his questions, he exclaimed, "That's the way I have seen myself all my life!" and he left the room. I rose from the table, and followed to another room where he was sitting facing the computer. I put my hand on his shoulder. "Have you been waiting all these years for a Dad who would meet you in the driveway, and love you?"

"That's exactly what I have always wanted," he replied.

"Well, you have one now," I said through tears, as we embraced.

Jesus said, *"I am the resurrection and the life. He who believes in Me, though he may die, he shall live.* (John 11:25)

> *"Blessed are the meek, for they shall inherit*
> *the earth."* (Matthew 5:5)

---

[52] An unpublished poem by Bardo Wiens. Used with permission

I REPENT OF THE FALSE 'SELF' THAT REVELED IN CO-DEPENDENCE AND IDOLATRY

The New Testament concept of repentance is often defined as a turning around, a changing of the mind. In the Old Testament, the concept is grander. I not only turn around, but I return to the place where I left the designated path, and then I carry on my journey. In short, I get back on track.

So what does it mean to get back on track? When a lawyer questioned Jesus about the greatest commandment in the Law, Jesus responded,

> *"You shall love the LORD your God with all your heart, with all your soul, and with all your mind.' "This is the first and great commandment. "And the second is like it: 'You shall love your neighbor as yourself"'* (Matthew 22:37-39)

It is my firm conviction that we can only love after we have received love. If I try to love you before I have received love, I will offer you my emptiness, and manipulate you into filling it. If you don't, I will write you off. John, the apostle, writes, *"We love Him because He first loved us"*. (1John 4:19) The track to be on is that which concentrates on receiving the love of God in our hearts, and then letting that love flow on to others.

If, indeed, it is as a little child, that the deception begins, and I am deceived into idolatry – doing it my way because I don't trust God – then repentance may well involve going back to reconcile with the lost inner child, so the child will be free to love and proceed along the journey back to authenticity, lest one become double-minded. (James 1:8) Jesus said,

> *"No one puts a piece from a new garment on an old one; otherwise the new makes a tear, and also the piece that was taken out of the new does not match the old."* (Luke 5:36)

Similarly, one does not try to build anything meaningful on a foundation that is compromised. The adult and the child must be on the same page.

> *"Blessed are those who hunger and thirst for righteousness, for they shall be filled"* (Matthew 5:6)

WHAT DOES IT MEAN TO BE HOLY?

If, indeed, I was born a holy and gifted individual, then to be authentic is to be original. But, I was deceived and led astray, and my 'self' was perverted. With my resurrection, however, my authenticity is restored. I am again holy. Even the word 'sanctification', which is often used in context with holiness, means 'to be set aside to fulfill an original purpose.' Might I therefore, suggest the following:

Holiness is…

- having the image and likeness of God restored in me through Jesus,
- freeing me to enjoy deeply meaningful love relationships with my Heavenly Father and others,
- and finding joy in the expression of my unique gifts and abilities in those relationships,
- thus celebrating God's amazing unique and original design for me.

There is a tendency on the part of those practicing the Christian religion to put strong emphasis on the need for integrity. Hence, it becomes a goal of their lives, and it is worshiped. I remember the day when the only compliment I could accept was that I had integrity. It was forcefully brought to my mind after I had purchased a large farm tractor in a community some thousand kilometers from home. The salesman told me he had checked with some businessmen back home, and they had reported that I was, "as honest as the day is long." Wow, did that feel good. In my own mind I had truly become 'Mr. Integrity'. I could really enjoy worshipping at that shrine.

I have since repented. I no longer believe that integrity is something to strive for. If you strive for it you will never attain it. It is much like joy – work for it, and it eludes you. However, both integrity and joy are by-products of authenticity. If you are authentic, you will have both – it's a package deal – and they come at no extra charge.

"Blessed are the merciful, for they shall obtain mercy." (Matthew 5:7)

WHAT DOES IT MEAN TO BE ACCOUNTABLE?

Some time ago, I wanted to sell some items, so I had a sign made. I went down to a local sign shop, gave the specifications, and asked for a ballpark estimate. When the sign was completed, I went back in to pick it up, only to find that the price had risen some seventy five per cent. I was a bit surprised, and mentioned to the clerk serving me that I had expected the price to be closer to the quote. She immediately summoned the manager. I expressed my surprise to him, and he responded quietly, "that quoting signs is not an exact science." So I suggested we split the difference, to which he agreed, but said he would need to change the bill in the computer. By this time I was not comfortable with my posturing, so I suggested I would pay the whole bill, which he allowed me to do. I went home with the sign, but a day later my conscience was nagging me. I had not valued his work as highly as he had, and wondered if he might be feeling that I was not valuing him.

So back to his office I went to apologize. When I came in the door, he immediately brought out my payment, and said he had not put it through because he was not expecting the whole amount. I apologized for my attitude and suggested he feel free to put the payment through. We chatted for a few minutes, and then I told him I needed to change the sign because the circumstances had changed. He immediately volunteered to redo the section I mentioned – at no charge. I thanked him. That day I left much more at ease than I had the previous day.

Was I being accountable – liable to be called to account? That depends on what the question means. Was I being accountable to get as much money in my bank as possible – in short to demand my own rights? I do not think so. Was I being accountable to maintain a good relationship with a businessman I enjoy – to extend grace? Perhaps. I am looking forward to going back to do more business. I would recommend him to my friends. I suspect that if we are going to be called to give an account, we need to set our priorities as to what is really important. Was I being accountable to value him as a man, made in the image and likeness of his Creator? I hope so. Was I being accountable to incarnate the love of Jesus to him as a fellow traveler? I pray so.

Jesus once told an intriguing story about accountability.

> *"When the Son of Man comes in His glory, and all the holy angels with Him, then He will sit on the throne of His glory. "All the nations will be gathered before Him, and He will separate them one from another, as a shepherd divides his sheep from the goats. "And He will set the sheep on His right hand, but the goats on the left. "Then the King will say to those on His right hand, 'Come, you blessed of My Father, inherit the kingdom prepared for you from the foundation of the world: 'for I was hungry*

and you gave Me food; I was thirsty and you gave Me drink; I was a stranger and you took Me in; 'I was naked and you clothed Me; I was sick and you visited Me; I was in prison and you came to Me.' "Then the righteous will answer Him, saying, 'Lord, when did we see You hungry and feed You, or thirsty and give You drink? 'When did we see You a stranger and take You in, or naked and clothe You? 'Or when did we see You sick, or in prison, and come to You?' "And the King will answer and say to them, 'Assuredly, I say to you, inasmuch as you did it to one of the least of these My brethren, you did it to Me.' (Matthew 25:31-40)

This group was so in love with God and mankind, that they did not know when they had done a loving act. It was part of their nature. They had received love freely, and had freely passed it on. Hence, when they were called to account, they were not expecting any rewards. But they were well rewarded, having chosen their priorities wisely. This, for me, is a picture of the 'Grace with Truth' crowd – true celebrants of God's love.

"Then He will also say to those on the left hand, 'Depart from Me, you cursed, into the everlasting fire prepared for the devil and his angels: 'for I was hungry and you gave Me no food; I was thirsty and you gave Me no drink; 'I was a stranger and you did not take

*Me in, naked and you did not clothe Me, sick
and in prison and you did not visit Me.'
"Then they also will answer Him, saying,
'Lord, when did we see You hungry or
thirsty or a stranger or naked or sick or in
prison, and did not minister to You?' "Then
He will answer them, saying, 'Assuredly, I
say to you, inasmuch as you did not do it to
one of the least of these, you did not do it to
Me.' "And these will go away into
everlasting punishment, but the righteous
into eternal life."* (Matthew 25:41-46)

This group thought they were being accountable. It
was not that they had done no merciful acts. They had
kept a record of their good deeds, and done them
faithfully - but because they were not authentic, their
motives were not pure. So when they were called to
account, they had difficulty realizing that they had totally
missed the mark. This is typical, of the 'Right vs. Wrong'
crowd – the practitioners of Christian Religion. I must
confess a deep trepidation as I write this last sentence. God
forbid that any should be in that category.

My first encounter with a pastor who seemed to
follow the goat's paradigm happened one night when I
was called to a meeting at the church I was attending. The
pastor, with a witness present, wanted to know why I was
slandering the church to the people of the neighborhood.
Wow! I did not know that I had been doing that, so I asked
for examples. He would reveal none. Then I asked for his
information source. I thought that if we could talk with the

source of the rumor, perhaps we could resolve the situation. He refused to divulge the source, saying it was confidential. Now we were in a dilemma. If I were slandering the church unawares, how could the situation be resolved if no one would explain the problem?

Actually, being my first encounter of this type, I took it very seriously. Just thinking about it made me shake, so prior to the next meeting, I went to see my medical doctor. I thought I needed some sedation to calm my shakes. Upon his query, I explained the situation. He listened intently. Then with a direct look at me, he said, "I will give you the medication. But, I will offer you a better solution as well. Tell your pastor to 'go to hell.'" I'm sure my shocked stare rather amused him.

I did not give my pastor that message. On reflection, I have come to the conclusion that he was free to make that choice for himself. But the deception is so clever, he may not have been aware of his choice. If indeed, his attitude puts him among the 'goats', I weep for him. I would rather warn him of his impending doom.

> *"Blessed are the pure in heart, for they shall see God."* (Matthew 5:8)

WHAT DO YOU SEE IN OTHER PEOPLE?

Journal entry – March 20: I met Jesus today – working as a waitress in a little restaurant in a prairie town.

My wife and I had been on the road for some eight hours of a twelve-hour road trip. It was mid- afternoon, and we were ready for a little break – maybe coffee and a piece of pie. We drove down the street, passing numerous fast food places and were about to give up when we came to a family restaurant.

As we sat down, the waitress approached – young, capable and friendly. But there was something else about her that caught our attention, something deeper, more to be felt than seen. They didn't have any pie either. But they did have cheesecake. Somehow that did not meet our fancy. "What about coconut cream banana cake? Had we ever experienced coconut cream banana cake?" she asked. Actually we hadn't so she brought a piece to show us. That did it. She brought two pieces with coffee, and what a satisfying experience it was!

Later, as we chatted, she told us a bit about her life. Her mother had MS, and was facing the possibility of being confined to a wheel chair. They were being advised to refit the house with ramps.

Then she told us of pain attacks she, herself, was having in her lower back – kidney stones, she said. The pain had come and gone for some time, but the stones would not respond to treatment – they would not crush nor dissolve. Now her gall bladder was also being affected. Her physician had informed her that after surgery she, herself, might well be confined to a wheel chair for up to six weeks. She was not complaining – just letting us in on what was going on in her life in her own quiet, confident way.

How our hearts went out to her! I had never before in this type of a situation felt such a strong urge to offer her a hug – to tell her we cared. But we had just met. Moments before, we had been total strangers. Now we felt an indescribable bond with this young lady – it appeared to be mutual. How we longed for her total restoration.

Leaving was difficult, waving to her as she stood watching from the door. We were deeply touched, and powerfully enriched. What an honor to be let into the inner recesses of one made in the image and likeness of her Creator. That encounter became the highlight of the whole trip.

Journal entry – March 23: I met Jesus today – wearing the disguise of a former drug addict. He had been in and out of relationship with his wife for several years, but now appeared to be growing emotionally and spiritually. He wondered aloud, "What does it mean to love my wife? How does one really love?"

At a supper out, he had given his wife some tidbits off of his plate, because he wanted to share something he knew she liked – just because he wanted to. And yet he wrestled. Were his motives pure? It was a new gesture. He had never done this before. What a neat struggle, exploring what it means to love. Sometimes I feel like I might burst.

Journal entry – March 24: I saw Jesus today – driving, of all things, a Ford F250 pickup truck. He looked old. As he pulled into the parking spot, he maneuvered his pickup right next to the curb. I was intrigued. Then I found out why. His wife was a senior as well, and not very tall. In the absence of running boards, the curb provided an intermediate step to make mounting and dismounting easier for his wife. What a neat gesture. Jesus is so considerate. There is so much beauty around us!

Journal Entry – March 30: I saw Jesus, today, as a school liaison worker whose love changed the children in his care to the point that the administration, on seeing the results, began to adopt a more compassionate approach to dealing with troubled children.

Journal Entry – April 5: I saw Jesus again today – this time disguised as an employer who cared enough for his 'crack addicted' employee to pick him up, take him home, and spend time with him whenever he was being tempted to buy more product – no matter what time of day. His love is paying off positively in the employee's life, as he conquers his addiction.

What do you see when you encounter people? Mother Theresa, in her work among the poor of India, said she saw Jesus in all of the people to whom she ministered. At first glance, that may appear to be a preposterous statement. But I have come to see that the more I listen to people, the more I observe them, the more I, too, see Jesus in them. Just behind the exterior will be found one made in the image of God – you just need to be able to recognize it. And when you see it, you can rejoice that you are beginning to see what God intended to be seen in the creatures he created in his image.

Herein, I suggest, lies the most startling difference between the two paradigms. The right/wrong crowd is looking to see the devil in everything. The approach is, "What have you done wrong now?" It is a negative approach that is part of the deception. We don't even realize we are doing it. But those raised in this paradigm grow up with little self worth. Hence, they will perform to get a sense of value. And they become legalistic. Jesus would say they represent old wine in brittle wineskins.

When you are a truth seeker, however, you look for the truth in people – and the truth is that we are created in the image and likeness of our Creator. We, too, are creative. We, too, have dignity. But it is in our need to be affirmed that we must make a choice. If our affirmation is based solely on what people say about us, we will become performers and move toward a right/wrong attitude. If, however, we accept the affirmation God offers us,[53] we will know the truth about God and ourselves, and the truth will set us free – free to love and free to be loved. Free to see Jesus in others. Free to be fermenting wine in flexible wineskins.

> *"Blessed are the peacemakers, for they shall be called sons of God."* (Matthew 5:9)

A DOCTRINAL SUMMARY

Allow me to restate the doctrinal progression that can happen as we walk in grace with truth:

- God creates me in the womb for a specific purpose.
- I am holy – I am gifted.
- I yield to the deceiver.
- I lose transparency, I lose trust, I break relationship.

---

[53] See Appendix Three for Scriptures that affirm our identity.

- The unique creation I was designed to be, dies – I wear a mask.
- I reap painful consequences.
- The Father draws me to himself, and opens my heart to receive Jesus' love .
- Jesus resurrects me - My 'self' is restored.
- I repent of the idolatry that I reveled in as a co-dependent.
- I re-enter a relationship of transparency, trust and love with my Heavenly Father.
- I become authentic (holy), and my genuine humanity reflects God's likeness.
- I take responsibility for my actions and beliefs – I am accountable.
- I offer love and empathy – I have freely received, I freely give.
- I accept you the way you are – and see Jesus in you, even if you don't.

> *"Not that I have already obtained all this,"* St Paul says, *"or have already been made perfect, but I press on to take hold of that for which Christ Jesus took hold of me."* (Philippians 3:12)

I believe a fitting paraphrase of St. Paul's thought could read, "I do my best to clear the path so that God's amazing original design for me can be realized."

I suspect that Job, in his latter years, would have agreed.

CHAPTER SIX

Job: A Life in Transition

When the flower is crushed,
its fragrance is released.

"For we are to God the fragrance of
Christ among those who are being saved
and among those who are perishing."
(2 Corinthians 2:15)

There lived a man, the Bible says,[54]somewhere in the East, in an area known as Uz. His name was Job. He was very wealthy, and had a very diversified business plan. He owned seven thousand sheep, suggesting he was strongly into meat and wool production. He owned three thousand camels, presumably to operate a transportation network across the desert, perhaps being himself, involved in trade. In addition, he owned five hundred yoke of oxen, which would have been used in agricultural production and perhaps in commerce as well. He also owned five hundred donkeys, which would have served well, both in local transportation and commerce. Add to this a large number of servants to operate this empire, and we see Job as the greatest man among all the people of the East. Incidentally, he also had a family.

---

[54] Job 1:1

I mention family as an afterthought, because in the beginning of the story, that is the way Job treated them. Notice the narrative:

> *"And his sons would go and feast in their houses, each on his appointed day, and would send and invite their three sisters to eat and drink with them. So it was, when the days of feasting had run their course, that Job would send and sanctify them, and he would rise early in the morning and offer burnt offering according to the number of them all. For Job said, "It may be that my sons have sinned and cursed God in their hearts." Thus Job did regularly."* (Job 1:4-5)

Place yourself in their shoes. How would you feel having a dad who insisted on getting you up early whenever you spent time with your siblings, in order to make offerings in case you had sinned. It sounds like he did not trust them very much. Perhaps they even reacted to Dad's suspicions and acted in a way that made him feel justified in his actions. Teens will do that. But to the neighbors (and to many present-day theologians) this act would certainly stand to Job's credit as being a righteous man. But the children would have significance only because their righteousness would make Dad look good. Perhaps it is typical of religious parents you may know. Job may well be more modern than he appeared at first glance.

Now Job was running a large commercial empire and was obviously rather busy, so he had to schedule his time wisely. This is the only mention of how he spent time with his children. He did, however, have a fair bit of time for other people. Again, notice the narrative, as it records Job's words:

> "When I went out to the gate by the city,
> When I took my seat in the open square,
> The young men saw me and hid,
> And the aged arose and stood;
> The princes refrained from talking,
> And put their hand on their mouth;
> The voice of nobles was hushed,
> And their tongue stuck to the roof of their mouth.
> When the ear heard, then it blessed me,
> And when the eye saw, then it approved me;
> Because I delivered the poor who cried out
> The fatherless and the one who had no helper
> The blessing of a perishing man came upon me,
> And I caused the widow's heart to sing for joy
> I put on righteousness, and it clothed me;
> My justice was like a robe and a turban.
> I was eyes to the blind,
> And I was feet to the lame.
> I was a father to the poor,
> And I searched out the case that I did not know.
> I broke the fangs of the wicked,
> And plucked the victim from his teeth."
> (Job 29:7-17)

If you will recall the story of the sheep and the goats from a previous chapter, you will remember that the truly righteous did not remember doing any righteous deeds. The goats, however, remembered very well. It would appear that at this point Job would have fit in well with the goats – his identity is based on his charitable performance.

Another characteristic of self-righteousness, I would suggest, is the worship of integrity. Can you imagine being Job's wife? She had to live with his judgmental attitude toward her children. She had to live with a man who was doing so many good deeds outside the home, and yet we don't have any recorded time in the home. She could see through his hypocrisy, while he seemed totally blind to it. Consequently it is not surprising for her to ask him, "Are you still holding on to your integrity? Why not bless God, and let the façade die?" An alternate might be, "Do you still worship integrity? Why not curse your god and let it die?" The narrative actually puts it this way:

> Then his wife said to him, "Do you still hold fast to your integrity? Curse God and die!" But he said to her, "You speak as one of the foolish women speaks. Shall we indeed accept good from God, and shall we not accept adversity?" In all this, Job did not sin with his lips. (Job 2:9-10)

The narrative gives us the traditional interpretation. However, what creates some difficulty is the word 'barak' in the original. It can be interpreted as either, 'to bless', or 'to curse' depending on the context. If one sees Job's wife as a grouch, the translation "Curse God' would make sense. If, however, one see Job's wife as an emotionally healthy woman who sees the broader picture of what God wants to do in Job's life, she would want to bless what God was doing, and alternately, curse Job's false god, even if it meant severe loss for herself. I prefer the latter interpretation.

Notice also the response of Job, who *never sinned with his lips*, though we can only speculate as to where his *heart* was. True to form, he does not understand what she is saying, and associates her idea with those of foolish women. When one sees Job's attitude toward his children and his wife, it is not difficult to make some assessment of their home life. Job also displays his arrogance against those young men who mock him, whose fathers didn't even rate being with Job's dogs. [55]

And yet God, in speaking with Satan, calls Job blameless or perfect[56]. How so? The word in the original, 'tam' has to do with piety or performance of charitable acts, but not necessarily of pure motive. It is interesting that Job and Jacob[57] are the only men I can find in the Biblical record described by this word. Noah[58] was also described as perfect, but the original uses a different word, 'tamim.' This word implies truth in the whole being – a condition of the heart. It is used also to describe God, and is the word used in the admonishment 'to be perfect as God is perfect'.[59]

---

[55] Job 30:1-9
[56] Job 1:8
[57] Genesis 25:27
[58] Genesis 6:8
[59] Genesis 17:1, Deuteronomy 18:13,

When we first meet Job, it would appear that he is a rather arrogant, pious man – a religious man. If he were alive today one would expect him to be involved in the Christian religion, serving in the organization as a director or even as a pastor – a man who could teach you all about right and wrong, but very little about love. And yet, he was looking for God.[60] Somehow his piety did not produce that 'elusive something' he was looking for.

But the god he was looking for was a god of his own making – one that would rise up and fulfill all of Job's expectations, a god who would affirm that Job had been right all along. Job is not unlike another who stood on his own horse manure security cushion, expecting his universe to conform to his wishes. Meanwhile, something had to happen to open Job to the reality of who God really is.

So God, in his mercy, arranges to have Job lose everything he has – his children, his wealth, and his prestige. All he has left are his memories, and his wife – a wife who suggests that perhaps this would be a good time to give up his idolatry. He derides her for it.

Then who should show up but three old friends? I can well imagine that when Job and his cronies had met before, they had spent a great deal of time in theological debate. Immediately they begin to talk of what God should or should not do in this situation. One thing is certain – when four people in the right/wrong crowd get together to discuss theology, they will each be very sure of their own right beliefs. And if something comes up that they cannot deal with, they can always shift the blame to someone else.

---

[60] Job 19:26-27

And that is precisely what these folks do until they all realize no one is going to budge in his position. The three so-called friends agree that Job's problems are of his own making – he insists on his innocence, and blames God. Since God isn't entering the debate at this time, that position is fairly safe.

However, in the fray, Job makes a most interesting statement:

> *"...I know that my Redeemer lives, and that*
> *He shall stand at last on the earth; and after*
> *my skin is destroyed, this I know, that in my*
> *flesh I shall see God (Job 19:25-26)*

And that is exactly what happened. Job lost not only his possessions, but he also lost his skin.[61] Remember, in the Garden, God gave mankind the protection of skin so they could survive. Now by a miracle of God's mercy, Job, with his skin destroyed, survives to see God. What a neat picture of how we, too, must approach God, in total dependence.

> *Many things in me reside,*
> *That have filled my heart with pride*
> *Lord, I cast them all aside,*
> *And approach your throne empty-handed.*

> *All those tools that saw me through,*
> *Led me far away from You,*
> *Made me think that I could do,*
> *When indeed I was empty-handed.*

---

[61] See Appendix Two for additional thoughts on skin.

In my weakness you are strong
And You knew that all along
While I thought I'd do great things for You
Your love and mercy ever true
Would bring me surely to this place
Where I would fall upon my face
And just see what I am in You.

Oh, the poverty of pride,
That would make me leave Your side –
Lord, in shame I want to hide,
But you beckon me empty-handed.

Help me always to remain,
Now, as when this child first came,
Boasting only in Your name,
You use me best empty-handed.
So here I am – empty-handed.[62]

He wants our total reliance to be on him. As long as we are depending on something other than God to sustain us and meet our needs, we will hear about him, but we will never see him. But Job did see God. And this is how it happened.

While Job's friends had been busy expounding on Job's folly, a young man had joined them. He sat respectfully by, waiting while the older men spoke, perhaps hoping to learn something from the conversation. His name was Elihu, meaning 'He is my God.' How he must have wept as he listened to the callous speeches of

---

[62] Empty-Handed, lyrics written by Debbie Zepick, featured on her CD Gold and Silver - 1995. www.debbiezepick.com/gold.htm# Used with permission.

Job's friends, and observed Job in his pain. Now that there is silence, he begins to speak.

He reminds Job that as a mortal, he has been telling God how to act.[63] Then he goes on to suggest that Job really needs a mediator who will mediate between Job and God, and show him that God is righteous. Job's silence suggests that he is finally choosing to listen to someone else, and receive what he has to offer. Elihu affirms Job, but says that he has acted defiantly, and now has the choice - to turn from iniquity and serve God, or tough-it-out and die. He invites Job to give up his judgmental attitude, for, says he:

> *"He (God) is wooing you from the jaws of distress to a spacious place, free from restriction, to the comfort of your table laden with choice food"* (Job 36:16, NIV)

Job says not a word, but as he listens, somehow Elihu's words prepare him to listen to God - and God speaks.

As God speaks of his creative power, Job realizes that indeed, as a human he cannot fathom God, nor tell him what to do. He responds to God by saying,

> *"I know that you can do everything, and that no purpose of Yours can be withheld from You... Therefore I have uttered what I did not understand, things too wonderful for me, which I did not know. I have heard of You by*

---

[63] Job 33:8-12

*the hearing of the ear, but now my eye sees
You. Therefore I abhor myself, and repent in
dust and ashes."* (Job 42:2-3b,5-6)

So Job did see God, as he had predicted earlier, and the encounter changed him. As the book concludes we see him no longer arguing theology with his friends, but praying for them.[64] Then God not only restores his empire, but doubles it. His siblings and former friends come to visit and encourage him, and he has time to eat meals with them – suggesting some major feasting. His wife bears him seven more sons, and three more daughters. Now Job is a changed man – he has time for his children. In fact, we are told that he names his three daughters. The first he named Jemimah, meaning warm and affectionate dove. The second he named Kezia, or little cinnamon stick (at a time when cinnamon was more expensive than gold). The third he named Keren- Happuch or container of antimony (a highly prized eye shadow). In all the land there were no women to be found as beautiful as the daughters of Job – a tribute to their father's love. And at a time when women were not highly esteemed, he gave them an inheritance along with their brothers.

Quite a change this is from the dad who would wake his kids early to make sacrifice, just in case they had sinned. Indeed, the narrative concludes with Job living to enjoy his children, his grandchildren, his great grandchildren, and his great, great grandchildren. Then he died, having lived a full life.

---

[64] Job 42:10

So what made the difference for Job? His search for God in the beginning of the book reflects a rational approach to being godly. He spent his time not only helping the underdog, but also getting involved in community activities. He had heard about God, and he was going out of his way to please him. And just to be safe, Job kept track of his righteous acts. Unwittingly, he had become distracted by clutter.

But in all of this, he appears to have a longing to know God more personally – a longing that intensified as his troubles increased:

> *For I know that my Redeemer lives,*
> *And He shall stand at last on the earth;*
> *And after my skin is destroyed, this I know,*
> *That in my flesh I shall see God,*
> *Whom I shall see for myself,*
> *And my eyes shall behold, and not another.*
> *How my heart yearns within me!*[65]

He wanted a deep, personal experience with God. And God was willing to grant his request. But two things needed to be dealt with. Job needed to face the fact that his own personal efforts at righteousness would never accomplish anything except pride in his accomplishments. He also needed to open his mind to the possibility that there was more to life than what he could explain – he needed to accept mystery. To accomplish this, God eliminated the clutter, and then, through the pain, opened

---

[65] Job 19:25-27

Job's heart. Now Job could begin to appreciate a totally new dimension in life. He saw God.

When a person hears of God, he/she may become religious, and generate all manner of performance to try to become godly. But when one sees[66] God, he/she repents of efforts at being god, and allows God to do a miracle within – producing the very qualities that the heart longed for, but performance was unable to produce. He/she is restored in the image and likeness of the Creator.

---

[66] Job 42:5-6

Reflections on the Journey[67]

God takes you where you've asked to go
Along the path that's right...
It leads down through the valley,
And over mountain height.

But when the journey first begins,
You seem to walk alone,
Oft stumbling through the underbrush,
Oft bumping on a stone.

The heart cries out, "God, smooth the path.
A miracle I need!
Clear up this mess – smooth out the road,
I want to move with speed!"

God does not speak – the choice is mine...
Those mountains up ahead -
I want them gone! They look so steep.
Who'll smooth them out instead?

God does not speak. My faith grows small.
What god will smooth my trail?
Can this god help? Can that one fix?
I try them, but they fail.

---

[67] This poem was composed in 2000 by the author upon recovering from a terminal illness. It also reflects his journey from a terminal spiritual condition in the 'Right vs. Wrong' paradigm toward 'Grace and Truth'.

BEYOND THE CLUTTER

"Lord, Lord," I cry, "forgive my sin…
It is idolatry!
You made the earth – You choose my path,
I'll walk it now with thee.

And now he speaks – the Silent One,
"Just take my hand, you'll see
I AM the God who made the earth,
You walk this path with me."

I see the battle clearer now –
It's all about control…
Am I the captain of my ship?
The master of my soul?

The battle's won – I rest in peace
No matter what may be.
My hand within the Savior's hand
He'll walk the path with me.

The storm begins – the body's lashed
As though onto a tree.
What matter now? It's only flesh –
The spirit soars on free!

I feel his presence deep within,
He speaks so lovingly,
"My son." He says, "I've waited long
To spend this time with thee."

"You've been so busy rushing round,
You wouldn't take my rest.
But now you've spent this time with me –
Which do you think is best?"

REFLECTIONS ON THE JOURNEY

I'm overwhelmed! My heart cries out,
"Dear Lord, how can this be?
The Creator of the Universe
Has taken time for me...

To shape my thoughts, to mold my heart,
To give me my request...
To make the man I want to be
Who'll learn to love - and rest!"

As I look back new meaning comes
I want to sing and shout...
When Jesus walked this path with me
We took the scenic route!

APPENDIX ONE
HEART, HEAD, GUT

All Scripture references are from *The King James Version* (Cambridge: Cambridge) 1769. The relevant words have been underlined where modern translation has rendered them unrecognizable.

THE HEART CAN...

Psalm 105:25	He turned their <u>heart</u> to hate his people,
Genesis 42:28	and their <u>heart</u> failed *them,*
Exodus 4:21	I will harden his <u>heart,</u>
Deuteronomy 4:9	lest they depart from thy <u>heart</u>
Deuteronomy 7:17	If thou shalt say in thine <u>heart</u>
1 Samuel 16:7	the LORD looketh on the <u>heart.</u>
Esther 6:6	Now Haman thought (spoke) in his <u>heart,</u>
Job 38:36	who hath given understanding to the <u>heart?</u>
Psalm 101:2	with a perfect <u>heart</u> ("blameless; sincerity; entire; whole; complete; full.")
Proverbs 2:10	wisdom entereth into thine <u>heart</u>
Proverbs 4:23	Keep thy <u>heart</u> with all diligence;

Ecclesiastes 2:10	I withheld not my <u>heart</u> from any joy;
Jeremiah 9:14	have walked after the imagination (lust, twisted-ness, stubbornness, hardness) of their own <u>heart,</u>
Jeremiah 17:10	I the LORD search the <u>heart</u>
Jeremiah 17:9	The <u>heart</u> *is* deceitful above all *things*, and desperately wicked
Ezekiel 27:31	with bitterness of <u>heart</u>
Matthew 15:18-19	But those things which proceed out of the mouth come forth from the <u>heart;</u> and they defile the man. For out of the <u>heart</u> proceed evil thoughts, murders, adulteries, fornications, thefts, false witness, blasphemies
Matthew 5:8	Blessed *are* the pure (cleansed, spotless) in <u>heart</u>
Matthew 22:37	Jesus said unto him, Thou shalt love the Lord thy God with all thy <u>heart,</u> and with all thy soul, and with all thy mind.
John 16:6	sorrow hath filled your <u>heart.</u>
Acts 11:23	with purpose of <u>heart</u> they would cleave
Romans 5:5	the love of God is shed abroad in our <u>hearts</u>
Romans 10:10	For with the <u>heart</u> man believeth unto righteousness;
Colossians 3:15	And let the peace of God rule in your <u>hearts,</u>

Ephesians 6:6	doing the will of God from the <u>heart</u>;
Ephesians 3:17	That Christ may dwell in your <u>hearts</u> by faith;
Colossians 3:21	in singleness (sincerity, simplicity, bountiful) of <u>heart</u>
Hebrews 4:12	intents of the <u>heart</u>
1 Peter 1:21	*see that ye* love one another with a pure <u>heart</u> fervently

THE MIND CAN...

Mark 12:30	And thou shalt love the Lord thy God with all thy heart and with all thy soul, and with all thy <u>mind</u>), and with all thy strength:
Luke 1:51	he hath scattered the proud in the imagination of their <u>hearts</u>
Ephesians 1:18	The <u>eyes of your understanding</u> being enlightened;
Ephesians 2:3	fulfilling the desires of the flesh and of <u>the mind</u>;
Ephesians 4:18ff	Having the <u>understanding</u> darkened,
2 Peter 3:1	I stir up your pure <u>minds</u> by way of remembrance
Luke 24:45	Then opened he their <u>understanding</u> that they might understand the scriptures,

Romans 1:28	God gave them over to a reprobate <u>mind,</u>
Romans 7:23	warring against the law of my <u>mind,</u>
Romans 7:25	So then with the <u>mind</u> I myself serve the law of God;
Romans 12:2	be ye transformed by the renewing of your <u>mind,</u>
Romans 14:5	Let every man be fully persuaded in his own <u>mind.</u>
1 Corinthians 1:10	be perfectly joined together in the same <u>mind</u>
1 Corinthians 2:16	But we have the <u>mind</u> of Christ.
Ephesians 4:23	And be renewed in the spirit of your <u>mind;</u>
Philippians 4:7	the peace of God, which passeth all <u>understanding,</u>
Colossians 2:18	vainly puffed up by his fleshly <u>mind,</u>
2 Thessalonians 2:2	That ye be not soon shaken in <u>mind,</u>
1 Timothy 6:5	disputings of men of corrupt (thoroughly rotting) <u>minds,</u>
Revelation 13:18	Let him that hath <u>understanding</u> count the number of the beast:
Revelation 17:9	here *is* the <u>mind,</u> which hath wisdom

THE GUT (SPLEEN, TRANSLATED AS BOWELS) CAN...

Luke 1:78	Through the tender (bowels of mercies) <u>mercy</u> of our God
2 Corinthians 6:12	ye are straitened (pressed for room) in your own <u>bowels</u>
2 Corinthians 7:15	his <u>inward affection</u> (bowels) is more abundant toward you,
Philippians 1:8	I long after you all in the <u>bowels</u> of Jesus Christ.
Philippians 2:1	if any <u>bowels</u> and mercies, 2Fulfil ye my joy,
Colossians 3:12	Put on therefore, as the elect of God, holy and beloved, <u>bowels</u> of mercies,
Philemon 7	the <u>bowels</u> of the saints are refreshed by thee,
Philemon 12	receive him, that is, mine own <u>bowels</u>:
Philemon 20	refresh my <u>bowels</u> in the Lord.
1 John 3:16	seeth his brother have need, and shutteth up his <u>bowels</u> *of compassion*

THE GUT (BOWELS) CAN...

Genesis 43:14	And God Almighty give you <u>mercy</u> (bowels)
Genesis 43:30	his <u>bowels</u> did yearn upon his brother

Genesis 49:25	blessings of the breasts, and of the <u>womb</u>
Deuteronomy 13:17	shew thee <u>mercy </u>(bowels), and have compassion upon thee
1 Kings 3:26	for her <u>bowels</u> yearned upon her son
1 Kings 8:50	give them <u>compassion</u> (bowels) before them
Psalm 106:46	He made them also to be <u>pitied</u> (bowels)
Psalm 145:9	The LORD *is* good to all: and his <u>tender mercies</u> (bowels) *are* over all
Daniel 1:9	God had brought Daniel into favor and <u>tender love</u> (bowels) with the prince

THE GUT (KIDNEYS TRANSLATED AS REINS) CAN:

Job 16:13	He pierces my <u>heart </u>(kidneys), and does not pity
Job 19:27	Whom I shall see for myself… though my <u>reins </u>(kidneys) be consumed within me
Psalm 7:9	…God trieth the hearts and <u>reins</u> (kidneys)
Psalm 16:7	I will bless the LORD, who hath given me counsel: my <u>reins</u> (kidneys) also instruct me…
Psalm 26:2	Examine me …try my <u>reins</u> (kidneys) and heart
Psalm 73:21	…my heart was grieved, and I was pricked in my <u>reins </u>(kidneys)

Psalm 139:13	For thou hast possessed my <u>reins</u> (kidneys)
Proverbs 23:16	Yea, my <u>reins</u> (kidneys) shall rejoice, when thy lips speak right things
Jeremiah 11:20	…that triest the <u>reigns</u> (kidneys)
Jeremiah 12:2	…thou art near in their mouth, and far from their <u>reins</u> (kidneys)
Jeremiah 17:9	I the LORD search the heart, I try the <u>reins</u> (kidneys)
Jeremiah 20:12	O LORD of hosts, that triest the righteous, and seest the <u>reins</u> (kidneys) and the heart….
Lamentations 3:13	He hath caused the arrows of his quiver to enter into my <u>reins</u> (kidneys)
Revelation 2:19	…and all the churches will know that I am he which searcheth the <u>reins</u> (kidneys) and heart

APPENDIX TWO
SKIN FOR SKIN

"So Satan answered the LORD and said,
"Skin for skin! Yes, all that a man has he
will give for his life." (Job 2:4)

The phrase "skin for skin" has long puzzled theologians, and is oft thought of as a part of a longer saying that has been lost to antiquity. But perhaps it is not as obscure as one might think.

Skin is an amazing thing. It is a continuous protective covering, approximately twenty-two feet square on the adult and weighing about one sixth of the body weight. The epidermis, or outer layer, weighs some 500 grams. Gitt suggests the skin,

"is a (nearly) watertight covering which protects all body tissues from physical damage. At the same time the skin is a highly sensitive sense organ, which can simultaneously detect various stimuli that can be quite independent of one another.

Touching is ten times as strong as verbal or emotional contact. If touching were not pleasant, living things would not procreate. If we did not enjoy touching and caressing, there would be no sex,"[68]

Unbroken skin is one of our most effective defences, not only protecting passively, but also actively destroying invading infective agents. *"Normal flora, harmless bacteria that lives on the skin, protect the body by attacking harmful bacteria that try to take up residence."[69]* In addition, the skin protects the body from physical abrasions, bacterial invasion, dehydration, and ultraviolet radiation. The epidermis is constantly being rubbed off (partially in the form bath-tub ring) carrying with it any invaders, which may have taken up residence.

The tips of the fingers are so sensitive to projections they can detect a sharp point even if it stands only ten microns (a micron is a millionth part of a meter) above the surrounding surface.

This is the covering that God gave to Adam and Eve in the garden before they were expelled. They had been living in the garden (literally, a protective enclosure allowing for voluptuous living and sensual delights) until they chose to abuse the privileges they had been enjoying. This had been their private resort. And though they had been commanded to take dominion over the animals, the deceiver in a snake's body entered the sanctuary. Obviously Adam had already relinquished control as the serpent tempted his wife.

[68] Werner Gitt, <u>The Wonder of Man,</u> (Bielefeld, Germany: Christliche Leteratur-Verbretung e.V., 1999) p. 41
[69] Alan L. Gillen, <u>Body by Design,</u> (Green Forest, AR: 2003) Master Books, p. 126

The deceiver wanted them dead because of what they represented in a cosmic battle he was fighting with God – a battle that we do not fully understand. And indeed, it appeared that he had won the day.

However, God had other plans. Knowing mankind needed protection to live outside the garden, he provided it with skin. The protection was so natural and adequate, that mankind pays very little attention to its maintenance, except to oil it, wash it, paint it, tattoo it – all actions that have to do with putting on a pleasing appearance.

The deceiver, on the other hand, did not forget. He well knew of the deeper values of the skin, and what it had cost him in the battle. So when God presented him with a suitable opportunity in the person of Job, he requested a return to garden protection conditions in a post-garden world. "Skin for skin!" I suspect he was saying to God, "Adam and Eve were mine – they were dead. But you preserved the race by offering them skin. Now remove Job's skin, and see if he survives."

And God said, *"Behold, he is in your hand, but spare his life."* And that is precisely what happened – his skin is destroyed, but Job survives. Not only survives, but is reborn as his heart is opened to receive and offer love. Had the deceiver been as clever as he thought he was, he likely would not have accepted God's challenge.

So the message is clear. We have been given protection by God to survive in a hostile world. But even when the chips are down, and it appears that normal protection is removed, God is still able, not only to sustain, but to rebirth relationship with himself and those around us. The question is, "Are we willing to take the risk? Can we trust a God whom we do not see? Can we give up all that we think is essential to let God open our hearts? Or do we, like Job, hope he will do it for us?

He will. All he needs is an invitation. [70]

---

[70] Job 19:27 Job speaks, "*(God) whom I shall see for myself, and my eyes shall behold, and not another. How my heart yearns within me!*".

Appendix Three
WARM THOUGHTS FROM GOD

*"Come to Me, all you who labor and are heavy
laden, and I will give you rest."*
- Jesus (Matthew 11:28)

*"But as many as received Him, to them
He gave the right to become children of God,
to those who believe in His name:"*
- John (John 1:12)

*"Behold, what manner of love the Father has
bestowed on us, that we should be called
children of God!"*
- John (1 John 3:1)

*"So God created man in His own image;
in the image of God He created him;
male and female He created them."*
- Moses (Genesis 1:27)

*"For in Him (Jesus) dwells all the fullness of
the Godhead bodily; and you are complete
in Him, who is the head of all
principality and power."*
- St. Paul (Colossians 2:9-10)

"Blessed be the God and Father of our Lord Jesus Christ, who according to His abundant mercy has begotten us again to a living hope through the resurrection of Jesus Christ from the dead, to an inheritance incorruptible and undefiled and that does not fade away, reserved in heaven for you, who are kept by the power of God through faith for salvation ready to be revealed in the last time."
- St. Peter (1 Peter 1:3-5)

"Grace and peace be multiplied to you in the knowledge of God and of Jesus our Lord, as His divine power has given to us all things that pertain to life and godliness, through the knowledge of Him who called us by glory and virtue, by which have been given to us exceedingly great and precious promises, that through these you may be partakers of the divine nature, having escaped the corruption that is in the world through lust."
- St. Peter (2 Peter 1:2-4)

"My brethren, count it all joy when you fall into various trials, knowing that the testing of your faith produces patience. But let patience have its perfect work, that you may be perfect and complete, lacking nothing."
- St. James (James 1:2-4)

APPENDIX FOUR
CONTRASTING TWO PARADIGMS

RIGHT VS. WRONG:
The Blind Men and the Elephant[71]

It was six men of Indostan
To learning much inclined,
Who went to see the elephant,
(Though all of them were blind),
That each by observation
Might satisfy his mind.

The First *approached the elephant,*
And happening to fall
Against his broad and sturdy side,
At once began to bawl,
"God bless me! But the elephant
Is very like a wall!"

The Second, *feeling of the tusk,*
Cried, "Ho! What have we here,
So very round and smooth and sharp?
To me 'tis very clear,
This wonder of an elephant
Is very like a spear!"

---

[71] John Godfrey Saxe (1816-1887)
http://rack 1.ul.cs.cmu.edu/is/saxe/saxe0077.jpg?rs=1&br=1&br=1.0&rt=0

Beyond the Clutter

The Third *approached the animal,*
And happening to take
The squirming trunk within his hands,
Thus boldly up and spake,
"I see," quoth he, "the elephant
Is very like a snake!"

The Fourth *reached out an eager hand,*
And felt about the knee.
"What most this wondrous beast is like
Is mighty plain," quoth he;
" 'T is clear enough the elephant
Is very like a tree."

The Fifth, *who chanced to touch the ear,*
Said, "E'en the blindest man
Can tell what this resembles most;
Deny the fact, who can,
The marvel of an elephant
Is very like a fan."

The Sixth *no sooner had begun*
About the beast to grope,
Than seizing on the swinging tail
That fell within his scope,
"I see," quoth he, "the elephant
Is very like a rope."

And so these men of Indostan
Disputed loud and long,
Each in his own opinion
Exceeding stiff and strong.

142

CONTRASTING TWO PARADIGMS

Though each was partly in the right,
And all were in the wrong.

So oft in theologic wars,
The disputants, I ween,
Rail on in utter ignorance
Of what each other mean,
And prate about an Elephant
Not one of them has seen!

GRACE WITH TRUTH:
The Blind Men and the Elephant[72]

It was six men of Indostan
To learning much inclined,
Who went to see the elephant,
(Though all of them were blind),
That each by observation
Might satisfy his mind.

The First *approached the elephant,*
And happening to fall
Against his broad and sturdy side,
At once began to bawl,
"God bless me! But the elephant
Is very like a wall!"

---

[72] I have taken the liberty to modify the meaning of the poem slightly, by replacing the last two stanzas, suggesting the six men now operate out of a different paradigm.

The Second, *feeling of the tusk,*
Cried, "Ho! What have we here,
So very round and smooth and sharp?
To me 'tis very clear,
This wonder of an elephant
Is very like a spear!"

The Third *approached the animal,*
And happening to take
The squirming trunk within his hands,
Thus boldly up and spake,
"I see," quoth he, "the elephant
Is very like a snake!"

The Fourth *reached out an eager hand,*
And felt about the knee.
"What most this wondrous beast is like
Is mighty plain," quoth he;
" 'T is clear enough the elephant
Is very like a tree."

The Fifth, *who chanced to touch the ear*
Said, "E'en the blindest man
Can tell what this resembles most;
Deny the fact, who can,
The marvel of an elephant
Is very like a fan."

The Sixth *no sooner had begun*
About the beast to grope,
Than seizing on the swinging tail
That fell within his scope,

CONTRASTING TWO PARADIGMS

"I see," quoth he, "the elephant
I very like a rope."

And so these men of Indostan
Conferred to share their find.
As each view added to the truth
They pictured in their mind,
And lo, they saw the elephant
Despite them being blind.

And so within the Christian church
When differences arise,
A little grace could heal the wounds
That come as each one tries
To know the God of mystery,
Much hidden from their eyes.

ABOUT THE AUTHOR

The author has lived a rich and varied life, and is currently, with his wife of nearly half a century, enjoying life on a small farm in southern Alberta, not too far from the place where he discovered the comfort of horse-manure pillows in his youth. The road to his gate is paved, not with horse manure but with asphalt, making it easier for friends to drop by for a visit and some refreshment in any type of weather. The journey continues to be good.

It is his wish that the effort you have invested in reading this book has enriched your journey as well, and has been an encouragement to you as you move toward authenticity in your life.

He can be contacted at:

dewiens@canopycanada.net